Artisanal BURGER

50 ITALIAN TWISTS ON AN ALL-AMERICAN FAVORITE

MONDADORI

Food production is sustainable if it centers on the quality of people's lives, the protection of the environment and biodiversity and the ethics of production processes, while providing guidance in the choice of products and eating habits. In the meat chain, consumers need this information because they rely both on sustainability and the satisfaction of their expectations.

The quality of meat, whether red or white, is the result of a number of factors, such as the choice of breed and the methods of raising and feeding, which affect the welfare of animals and contribute to the definition of the organoleptic characteristics of the product.

For example, the slaughter age of cattle together with the figure for the live weight reached enables us to make certain assumptions about farming practices and so the quality of the meat. Hence asking farmers to state every step in the supply chain on the label, in a way clear and comprehensible to non-experts, is essential if we are to make informed choices.

On the other hand, it is important to ask consumers to be careful when shopping. Good meat is never the result of shortcuts. Consumers need to read the label carefully, understanding production systems and using their senses which are a valuable ally if well trained.

In this way we can say we are no longer only consumers but co-producers, responsible subjects who promote sustainable models and habits.

The co-producer's responsibility has to be oriented in many directions, especially towards the reduction of meat consumption, while favoring indigenous breeds and the environmental context in which they are traditionally set, with a willingness to pay an appropriate price for quality produce. In this way the co-producer can play an active role in defining a new style of consumption that respects the environment as well as the welfare of animal and those who raise them.

Nino Pascale President Slow Food Italy

Translation
Richard Sadleir

www.electaweb.com

This volume was printed for Mondadori Electa S.p.A.,
at Elcograf S.p.A., via Mondadori 15, Verona

MAKING THE BURGER HOLY

Long considered a simple fast food, the hamburger today has become a gourmet delight, with a selection of exclusive Italian ingredients, the finest meats, savory salumi, a great variety of fish and fresh vegetables, matched with sauces and condiments having a national and international appeal. This has made the burger a full, natural and genuine meal in Italy, not just bursting with flavor but also packed with nutritional quality. Now you can make tasty burgers easily at home too, and have fun preparing our 50 original recipes.

A TASTE TO CHERISH:
SACRED AS YOUR PLEASURE,
HOLY AS YOUR BURGER.

50 recipes. The philosophy of Ham Holy Burger is based strictly on the number 5 and its multiples. What's so special about 5? Because in the symbolism of numbers 5 stands for change, will power, genius, the emblem of those who are always on the move and reach out for ever new goals. Not surprisingly, the quintessence or "5th essence" is the highest of all elements. Like many ancient peoples, who always saw the number five as special, Ham, too, believes in its power, and always from a close affinity for this number conducts a continuing research into gastronomic trends, seeking to attain the height of pleasure through all 5 senses.

IN HARMONY
WITH YOUR
5 SENSES!

The most important part about making a
gourmet burger is choosing the ingredients. For classic beef burgers, the choice
goes straight to Scottona beef from pure-
bred Piedmontese heifers. A Scottona is a
young beef heifer, never impregnated, and
with extraordinarily tender flesh. It is finely
marbled with fat that melts in cooking to
release its delicious flavor. This is one of the
finest meats in Italy for taste and quality,
run in complete harmony with the seasons
of nature.

100% ITALIAN
QUALITY

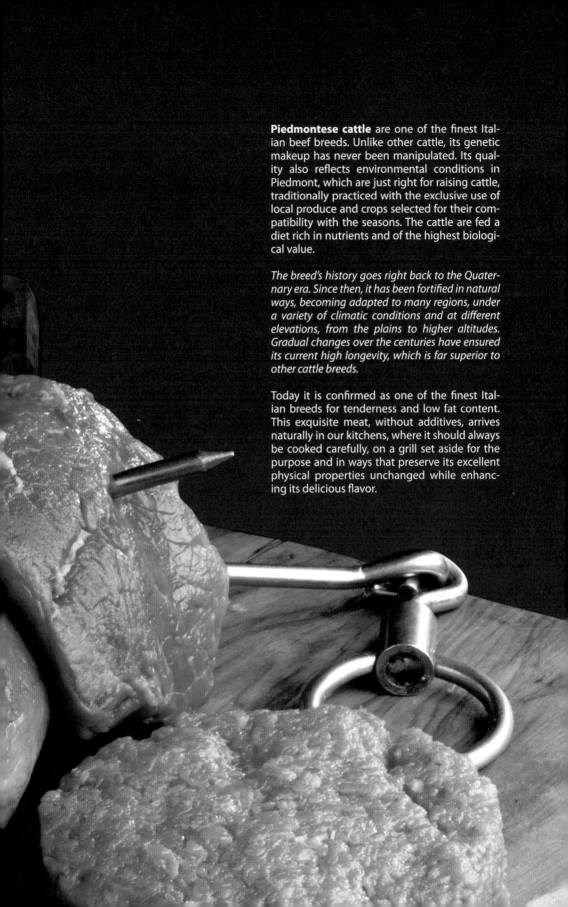

Piedmontese cattle are one of the finest Italian beef breeds. Unlike other cattle, its genetic makeup has never been manipulated. Its quality also reflects environmental conditions in Piedmont, which are just right for raising cattle, traditionally practiced with the exclusive use of local produce and crops selected for their compatibility with the seasons. The cattle are fed a diet rich in nutrients and of the highest biological value.

The breed's history goes right back to the Quaternary era. Since then, it has been fortified in natural ways, becoming adapted to many regions, under a variety of climatic conditions and at different elevations, from the plains to higher altitudes. Gradual changes over the centuries have ensured its current high longevity, which is far superior to other cattle breeds.

Today it is confirmed as one of the finest Italian breeds for tenderness and low fat content. This exquisite meat, without additives, arrives naturally in our kitchens, where it should always be cooked carefully, on a grill set aside for the purpose and in ways that preserve its excellent physical properties unchanged while enhancing its delicious flavor.

COOKING TIMES

Apart from its quality, the flavor of meat also depends on the way it is cooked. Raising the outer layer of the meat to temperatures around 140°C caramelizes the outer layers in what is called a Maillard reaction, imparting a rich flavor to the meat and giving it the typical roasted aroma. To measure the cooking time, the **temperature of the meat** has be measured at its heart, its deepest point, furthest from the surface, which is also where the temperature is lowest. Here the meat's temperature corresponds to different cooking points:

rare
45–50°C

medium
55–60°C

well done
75–85°C

FINGERTIP TEST

A simple way to measure the cooking point of a hamburger is known as the "fingertip test." All you need do is compare the consistency of the muscle in your hand right beneath your thumb to the different phases your burger goes through in cooking.

Open one hand and with the index finger of the other press the muscle just below the thumb: the consistency you feel matches **meat cooked rare.**

Then repeat, but this time join thumb and forefinger to feel the texture of **medium cooked meat.**

Finally, also join the middle and the ring fingers to measure the consistency of **meat cooked till it's well done.**

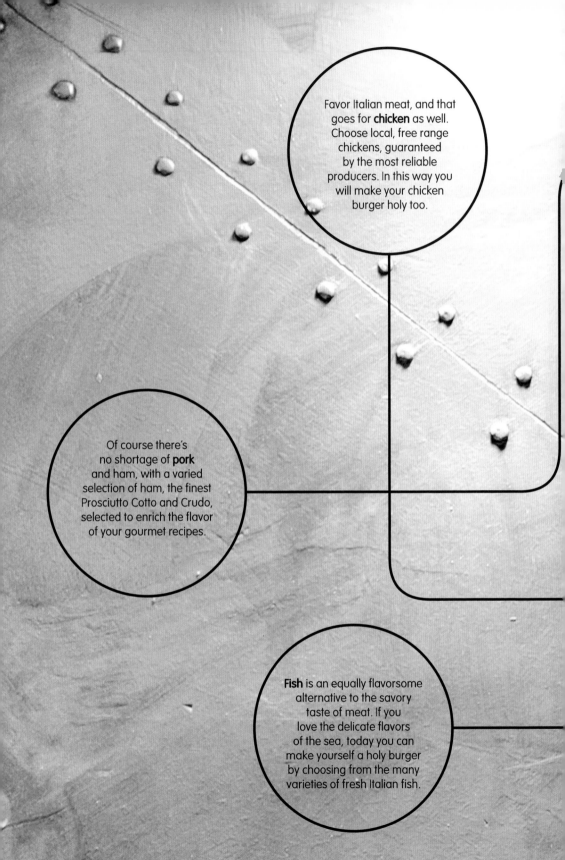

Favor Italian meat, and that goes for **chicken** as well. Choose local, free range chickens, guaranteed by the most reliable producers. In this way you will make your chicken burger holy too.

Of course there's no shortage of **pork** and ham, with a varied selection of ham, the finest Prosciutto Cotto and Crudo, selected to enrich the flavor of your gourmet recipes.

Fish is an equally flavorsome alternative to the savory taste of meat. If you love the delicate flavors of the sea, today you can make yourself a holy burger by choosing from the many varieties of fresh Italian fish.

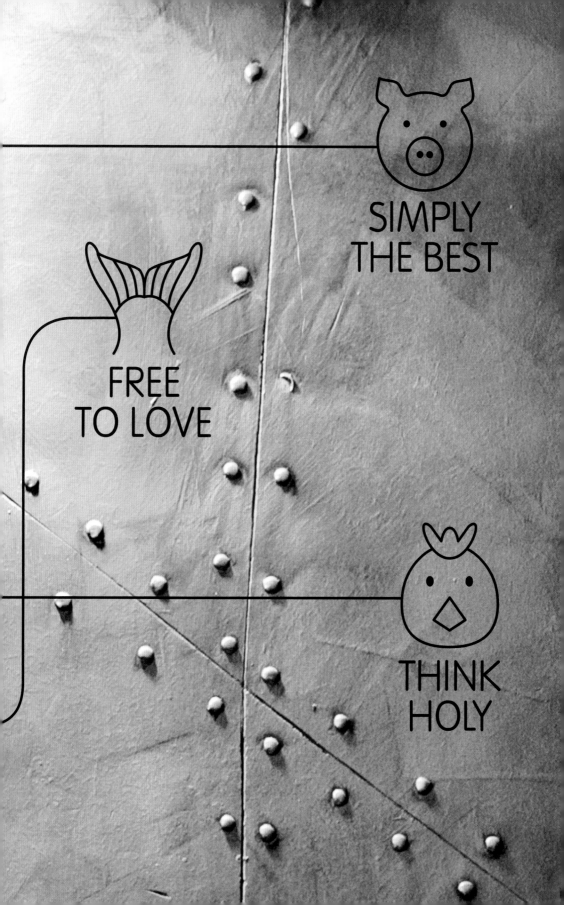

SIMPLY
THE BEST

FREE
TO LOVE

THINK
HOLY

HAND MADE BREAD

You can choose freely between different types of bread, but it should always be artisanal. Everything is holy that gives and preserves the pleasure of eating, like the goodness of Italian bread made from quality flour, naturally leavened and baked.

Bun

The bread roll used for burgers is known as a burger bun. It's not a traditional bread roll but should be made brioche style with a golden crust and compact fluffy crumb, so a mouthful can be bitten off easily together with all the filling. Imagine if it was chewy: it would take an effort to bite into it, threatening to spill out the ingredients. So it's important to make sure the bun is soft and fluffy and just right.

Then when you're making a burger and cuts your bun in half, you should always brown the two cut sides of the bun. In fact the key phase in making a burger is the browning of the bun in a skillet or on a smooth hotplate, at a moderate temperature of about 60°–70°C. Browning the bun not only makes it much more flavorful and fragrant but also crunchy inside, so the juices that run from the meat won't make it soggy or crumble, and it will stay firm to the last bite.

Make it yourself by following this easy recipe.

	makes 10 buns
500 g	**american or manitoba flour**
25 g	**brewer's yeast**
30 g	**milk**
50 g	**butter**
40 g	**sugar**
250 g	**plain yogurt**
1	**egg**
1	**egg yolk**
10 g	**fine salt**
	the brushing
2	**egg yolks**
30 g	**milk**

phase 1

To make a burger bun the first thing is to prepare the levain or starter.
Using a small bowl, dissolve the yeast in warm milk and then add 60 g of flour, cover with cling film and leave to rise for about an hour.

phase 2

In the mixer, use the dough hook to slowly knead the rest of the flour along with the sugar, egg and egg yolk, yogurt and salt. Once the volume of levain has doubled, mix it with the other ingredients, mixing rapidly for 10 minutes, then add the softened butter and knead the dough for another 10 minutes until it comes away easily from the bowl. Place the shaped dough on a lightly floured pastry board, cover it with a cloth and leave it to rise until its volume doubles.

phase 3

In a small bowl emulsify 2 egg yolks and the milk. Meanwhile, let the dough subside slightly, then slice it into pieces of 80 g each in the form of rounded buns. On a baking sheet lined with paper place the rolls in the oven about 2 cm apart to prevent them touching as they rise, cover with a cloth, let them rise for another hour, then brush them with part of the emulsion. Let them rise uncovered for another half hour until they plump out nicely. Then switch the oven to 180°C and brush the buns with the rest of the emulsion. Bake them in the preheated oven for about 15–20 minutes till they are golden brown.

OUR SAUCES
OUR SOUL

The sauces are much more than a condiment for our holy burgers. They are part of their very gourmet soul. They are tasty influence from the culinary traditions of various regions around the world. They have been tested by devising creative matches with spices, herbs, fruits and vegetables, cooked or puréed, with basic condiments such as mayonnaise, yogurt, mustard or other sauces, easily available but always of outstanding quality. Their role is to enhance the harmony or contrasts between the ingredients and heighten the pleasure of every single mouthful.

holy sauce

anchovy	1 fillet
mayonnaise	75 g
mustard seed	10 g
smoked barbecue sauce	150 g
ketchup	75 g
mustard	35 g
Mexican hot sauce or hot ketchup	15 g
Parmigiano Reggiano 24 months	15 g

In the blender cup add the anchovy, grated Parmigiano, a spoonful of smoked barbecue sauce and blend. Pour into a bowl, add all the other ingredients and mix with a spatula.

green tomato chutney

green tomatoes	800 g
brown sugar	250 g
ketchup with balsamic vinegar	50 ml
white onion	120 g
mustard	160 g
lime	2
sweet paprika	1 teaspoon
spicy paprika	1 teaspoon
thyme	1 sprig
garlic	1 clove
fine salt	
pepper	

Cut the green tomatoes in pieces and put them in a container so they shed their water. Cut the onion fine and put it in a saucepan with the tomatoes and all the other ingredients. Cook over low heat for half an hour until the liquids evaporate. Once cooked put in a carefully sterilized jar and keep.

rosemary sauce

mayonnaise	200 g
spreadable cream cheese like Philadelphia	100 g
cream	20 g
fresh needles of rosemary	5 g
extra-virgin olive oil	10 g

Mix the oil with the rosemary needles, then use a spatula to mix in the spreadable cream cheese. Add the cream, the oil and, if desired, a few spoonfuls of water. Put the mayonnaise in a bowl and mix in the cream cheese with rosemary. Store in the refrigerator.

basil mayonnaise

mayonnaise	250 g
Greek yogurt	400 g
basil	20 large leaves
extra-virgin olive oil	50 g
fine salt	1 pinch

Wash and dry the basil leaves, put them in the cup of the immersion blender, and zap them in bursts while adding a trickle of oil. Filter the whole, separating the oil from the basil.
In a bowl mix together the yogurt, a pinch of salt and mayonnaise with a spatula, adding a little water to dilute it if necessary. Add the filtered basil and mix well.

carrot and cumin mayonnaise

carrots	700 g
mayonnaise	300 g
garlic	½ clove
powdered cumin	1 teaspoon
extra-virgin olive oil	30 g
fine salt	

Peel the carrots, cut them into rounds, then cook till tender in a pan covered with water. Adjust for salt. When cooked, drain them carefully and zap them in the immersion blender with the garlic and oil to a smooth cream.
Add the powdered cumin and pour it all into a bowl. Once the mixture is cold mix in the mayonnaise using a spatula and store in the refrigerator.

tofu and curry sauce

zucchini	200 g
tofu	100 g
powdered onion	1 pinch
lemon	1
mild curry powder	1 teaspoonful
extra-virgin olive oil	40 g
fine salt	
white pepper	

Slice the zucchini into pieces, removing some of the pith from the middle. Heat the oil in a pan, add the zucchini and blanch them rapidly. Add enough water to just cover them and cook till soft. Allow to cool.
Crumble the tofu and add to the zucchini, then put everything in the blender cup. Blend adding the curry powder, a pinch of powdered onion and a little grated lemon zest. If the mixture is too thick add a little hot water. Adjust for salt and pepper, let it cool and store in the fridge.

tzatziki sauce

yogurt	400 g
cucumber	1
onion	10 g
garlic	1 clove
white wine vinegar	5 g
extra-virgin olive oil	10 g
fine salt	1 pinch

Trim, wash and seed the cucumber, then chop it finely and add salt to taste. Wrap it in a clean cloth and pat it lightly to dry. Chop the onion and garlic and mix them in a bowl with the cucumbers already carefully drained, then add the yogurt and mix with the oil and vinegar. Season with salt and store in the fridge.

green pepper and juniper mayonnaise

mayonnaise	200 g
whole milk yogurt	200 g
green pepper sauce	50 g
juniper berries	5 g

Chop the juniper berries small, then put the mayonnaise in a bowl and mix in the yogurt, green pepper sauce and chopped juniper berries.
If the mixture seems too thick dilute it with a few spoonfuls of water.

peanut sauce

peanut butter	500 g
mayonnaise	300 g

Warm 200 g of water and gradually add the peanut butter. Emulsify it and then add the mayonnaise. Mix them with a spatula. Store in a cool place.

yogurt sauce

mayonnaise	250 g
Greek yogurt	400 g
fine salt	1 pinch

Put the yogurt in a bowl with a pinch of salt and the mayonnaise. Mix well with a wooden spoon. Dilute if necessary with a little water.

redcurrant glaze

redcurrants	100 g
onion	50 g
garlic	½ clove
rosemary	1 sprig
brown stock	10 g
extra-virgin olive oil	15 g
butter	15 g
salt	1 pinch
pepper	1 pinch
mellow white grappa	

Warm the oil and butter in a pan and soften the finely chopped onion, garlic and rosemary. Add the redcurrants, crushing them with a fork then add the grappa and let it evaporate. Now add the brown stock dissolved in a glassful of warm water, reduce the stock to half its initial volume. Adjust for salt and pepper. Eliminate the rosemary and leave to cool.

honey and green pepper sauce

yogurt	200 g
green pepper sauce (see recipe)	50 g
honey	100 g
extra-virgin olive oil	50 g

Pour the yogurt in a bowl, add the green pepper sauce and honey and stir with a wooden spoon to blend in the oil. If the mixture is too thick dilute with a few spoonfuls of water and store in the fridge.

curry sauce

mayonnaise	150 g
yogurt	150 g
apple	1
onion	½
curry powder	5 g
butter, clarified if possible	30 g

Heat the butter in a pan, add the diced onion and apple. Cook till soft, adding water as needed, and mix in the curry powder. Once cooked allow to cool, then blend lightly and at the end mix in the yogurt and mayonnaise with a spatula.

caper mayonnaise

mayonnaise	200 g
salted capers	30 g
parsley	1 sprig

Desalt the capers by rinsing them in running water. Blend them with a spoonful of cold water and gently mix in the mayonnaise. Add the chopped parsley and then some further spoonfuls of cold water to dilute the sauce and make it smoother.

walnut pesto

walnuts	50 g
white bread	20 g
parsley	1 sprig
orange	1
garlic	1 clove
extra-virgin olive oil	10 g

To make the walnut pesto crumble the white bread and mix it with the walnuts, garlic, parsley, the orange peel and the 10 g of olive oil. Put everything in a cutter and blend in short bursts (to avoid heating the pesto), until you have a fairly coarse pesto.

old-style mustard mayonnaise

mayonnaise	200 g
mustard seeds	1 teaspoon
old-style mustard	40 g

Pour the mayonnaise into a container and combine all the ingredients, stirring gently. Add 80 g of water to dilute the mixture.
For a really tasty variant add 100 g of plain yogurt.

green pepper sauce

fresh cream	100 g
flour	1 pinch
white wine	1 sprinkle
green peppercorns	1 spoonful
shallot	1
butter	20 g
fresh tarragon	to taste
fine salt	

Simmer the shallot and keep the water it cooked in. Finely chop the shallot and put it in a small saucepan with the butter ready melted. Add the green peppercorns crushed with a meat mallet. Cook for at least a minute then deglaze with the white wine and add the flour, two or three spoonfuls of the shallot stock. Allow to thicken, then add the cream and finely chopped tarragon. Simmer, adjust for salt, then turn off the heat. Once cool store in the fridge.

citrus mayonnaise

mayonnaise	200 g
orange juice	40 ml
lemon juice	20 ml
orange	1
lemon	1
lime	1

Mix the orange and lemon juice, then gently add the mayonnaise and the zest of the orange, lemon and lime. Add a few spoonfuls of cold water to dilute the sauce and make it more fluid.

Potatoes are always a perfect match for burgers. And if you add a dipping sauce, their flavor will be new at every taste. You can choose between various ways of preparing and cooking potatoes: slicing them finely (as in packets of potato chips or crisps) to be fried in oil or wedges to be cooked in the oven. Then for kids, or all those who love their delicate flavor, there are also French fries to be eaten with or even in the bun.

FRESH FRIES
FRIENDS

fries**gourmet**

red-skinned potatoes
peanut oil

AROMATIC SALT (paprika salt)

sweet paprika	1 spoonful
spicy paprika	½ spoonful
double salt	1 spoonful
cumin	1 pinch
garlic powder	1 pinch

Quickly blend all ingredients. Then wash the potatoes, taking care they are about the same size. Dry them and put them whole on a baking sheet, on a layer of double salt. Roast at 180°C for about 50–60 minutes. They have to be still firm when cooked: to make sure stick a toothpick in them to check they are done. Once they are cooked let them cool and then cut them lengthways into wedges. Then heat plenty of peanut oil in a skillet or tall-sided pan (like a wok) to 170°C and fry the potatoes in small batches. Drain and let them absorb the excess oil, then sprinkle with aromatic salt.

fries**chips**

yellow-skinned potatoes
peanut oil
fine salt

To make fries you should use potatoes with firm yellow flesh. Cut them into thin slices about 1.5 mm thick, using a mandolin cutter or sharp knife. Then put them in a container and wash them carefully under running water until it runs clear. Alternatively soak them and change the water two or three times. Then store them in water and ice.
To fry use peanut oil, which has a high smoke point and does not alter the flavor. Use abundant oil in a high-sided skillet (like a wok).
The ideal temperature is 170°C for direct frying.
Drain carefully and fry in small batches, then place the fries on a sheet of kitchen paper to drain the oil. Add salt only at the end.

fries**stick**

yellow-skinned potatoes
peanut oil
fine salt

Start by cutting the potatoes into slices about 5 or 6 mm thick, then cut them into sticks and soak them in water, changing the water two or three times. Store them in water and ice. Bring the oil to 150°C and fry the potatoes until soft and very yellow. Then fry them again in a second skillet, raising the oil to 180°C to make them crispy and golden. Drain carefully, add salt and serve immediately.

Ham is the pioneer
of a new trend: through
a gourmet interpretation,
a global tradition
has become an Italian
excellence.

ITALIANS
DO IT
BURGER

holyburger

difficulty
EASY

patty
SCOTTONA BEEF

season
4 SEASONS

inspiration
ITALY / NORTH AMERICA

condiment
HOLY SAUCE

1	**bun**
1	**Scottona beef patty 180 g**
1 slice	**Sorrento beefsteak tomato**
3 slices	**fresh cucumber**
2-3 rings	**red onion**
1 leaf	**lettuce**
40 g	**holy sauce**
	butter
	extra-virgin olive oil
	fine salt

Lightly brush the patty with extra-virgin olive oil, make sure the grill is hot and cook the patty as desired.
Meanwhile, cut the bun in half, smear a little butter on the cut sides and brown them in a nonstick skillet. Put the base of the bun on a cutting board and place the patty on it with the lettuce, tomato, a pinch of salt, the cucumber and the onion rings. Then pour some of the holy sauce (see "Sauces") in the middle and spread the other half bun with the rest of the sauce. Cover the bun and pin it all together with a cocktail stick.

special guest
HOLY SAUCE

Our original recipe, created to season our international gourmet food with a wholly Italian flavor.

serve with
PALE LAGER BEER

clubburger

difficulty	patty	season	inspiration	condiment
EASY	SCOTTONA BEEF	SUMMER	ITALY	STRACCHINO SAUCE

1	**bun**
1	**Scottona beef patty 180 g**
40 g	**Stracchino cheese**
30 g	**Caciocavallo Podolico**
20 g	**fresh zucchini**
1 sprig	**wild arugula**
1 clove	**garlic**
1 sprig	**fresh thyme**
	butter
	extra-virgin olive oil
	fine salt
	pepper

Prepare the aromatic oil with garlic and thyme. Heat a nonstick skillet. Slice the zucchini thinly lengthways, blanch them brief in the hot pan and season with the aromatic oil.

Put the Stracchino in a bowl and dress it with a little olive oil, thyme and pepper, then mix it using a spatula and a trickle of water.

Brush the patty with a little oil, put it on the heated grill and cook as desired. Meanwhile cut the bun in half, spread a little softened butter on the cut sides and brown the two halves in a nonstick skillet.

Rest the base of the bun on a chopping board and add the arugula, patty, sliced zucchini and shavings of Caciocavallo. Finally smear the other half bun with the Stracchino sauce, cover the burger and pin it all together with a cocktail stick.

special guest
CACIOCAVALLO PODOLICO

This is a special cheese produced exclusively from the milk of Podolica cows, using traditional methods and only at certain times of the year. It is a noble cheese matured over long periods (5 or 6 years) which gives it a very distinctive taste, complex aromas redolent of the pastures and Mediterranean scrub and outstanding physical qualities.

serve with

PALE LAGER BEER

goodyburger

difficulty	patty	season	inspiration	condiment
HIGH	PORK	SPRING	ITALY / BRITAIN	SMOKY BARBECUE SAUCE

1	**bun**
1	**180 g pork patty**
30 g	**radicchio**
2–3 ring	**red onion**
30 g	**smoky barbecue sauce**
	butter
	extra-virgin olive oil

cheese cream

40 g	**Doomstone (English cheese)**
10 g	**cream**
5 g	**bourbon**
	pepper

sauté of cherries, sweet or sour

50 g	**fresh cherries, sweet or sour**
1	**red onion**
30 g	**balsamic vinegar ketchup**
1 sprig	**rosemary**
5 g	**extra-virgin olive oil**
	salt
	pepper

To make the Doomstone cream, put the cheese on a cutting board and chop it lightly with a knife, then place it in a bowl, stir in the bourbon, a teaspoonful of fresh cream and the pepper.

Prepare a sauté of sweet or sour cherries: pit the cherries. Slice the onion finely and sweat it in a skillet with a little olive oil and the rosemary, then add the pitted cherries. Add salt and pepper. Pour in a spoonful of balsamic vinegar ketchup and reduce.

Brush the patty lightly with oil and cook on the heated grill as desired.

Cut the bun in half, spread the cut sides with softened butter and brown them in a pan. Spread a little barbecue sauce on the bottom half of the bun and add the radicchio julienned, the onion rings, the patty, a spoonful of sautéed cherry and the Doomstone cream. Spread the other half of the bun with the rest of the barbecue sauce and cover the bun. Pin it all together with a cocktail stick and serve.

serve with
STOUT BEER

gleeburger

difficulty
HIGH

patty
CHICKEN

season
SPRING

inspiration
ITALY

condiment
MAYONNAISE CITRUS

1	**bun**
1	**180 g chicken patty**
2 slices	**Cheddar cheese**
1 slice	**artisanal smoked roasted ham**
1	**carrot**
1-2	**fennel**
10 g	**raisins**
a few	**onion**
1 sprig	**fennel seed**
30 g	**wild arugula**
	citrus mayonnaise
	butter
	extra-virgin olive oil

Prepare the colorful salad: trim and wash the arugula, then chop it coarsely. Cut the onion, carrot and fennel into julienne strips. Chop coarsely the fennel seed and raisins, first plumping them in warm water, and mix together with a spoonful of mayonnaise prepared with citrus fruits (see "Sauces") and keep in a cool place.
Brush the patty lightly with oil, put it on the heated grill and cook as desired. Place two slices of Cheddar on the patty and cover with the lid to melt the cheese. After a few minutes add half a slice of ham.
Meanwhile, cut the bun in half, spread it with softened butter on the cut sides and brown them in a nonstick pan.
Put the base of the bun on a cutting board and add the arugula, the rest of the ham, the patty and the colorful salad. Spread the other half of the bun with a veil of citrus mayonnaise and cover the bun. Pin everything together with a cocktail stick.

serve with
PILSNER BEER

5

loungeburger

difficulty
MEDIUM

patty
SCOTTONA BEEF

season
WINTER

inspiration
ITALY

condiment
GREEN PEPPER SAUCE

1	bun
1	Scottona beef patty 180 g
20 g	Prosciutto Crudo di Parma 18 months Doppia Corona
20 g	Provolone Auricchio Stravecchio Scorzanera cheese
2	meadow mushrooms
2 leaves	lettuce
30 g	lemon juice
	truffle oil
	green pepper sauce
	butter
	extra-virgin olive oil
	salt
	black pepper

Wipe the mushrooms with a moist cloth, remove the stalks and sprinkle with a little lemon juice. Cut into thin slices and season with a little olive oil, salt and black pepper.
Brush the patty lightly with oil, put it on the heated grill and cook as desired.
Meanwhile, cut the bun in half, spread the cut sides with a little softened butter and brown them in a nonstick skillet.
Put the base of the bun on a cutting board, spread with a little green pepper sauce, add the lettuce, the patty, a trickle of truffle oil, the slivers of Provolone and slices of Prosciutto Crudo. Spread the rest of the green pepper sauce on the other half of the bun, cover the burger and pin everything together with a cocktail stick.

 serve with
MORELLINO RED WINE

keepburger

difficulty
MEDIUM

patty
SCOTTONA BEEF

season
WINTER

inspiration
FRANCE / ITALY

condiment
ROSEMARY SAUCE

1	**bun**
1	**Scottona beef patty 180 g**
30 g	**Bûche de chèvre**
	(French cheese)
2 slices	**Italian Speck**
2 leaves	**red spumiglia lettuce**
1	**fresh fig**
30 g	**rosemary sauce**
	butter
	extra-virgin olive oil
	onion sauté
100 g	**brown onion**
1 sprig	**fresh thyme**
	white wine
	extra-virgin olive oil
	fine salt
	pepper

Prepare the rosemary sauce (see "Sauces").
For the sauté warm a little oil in a skillet, add the onions and thyme with salt and pepper to taste, cover and sweat the onions. Now cover the onions with the wine and let it evaporate, then cook for a few minutes and keep the sauté warm.
Brush the patty lightly with oil, put it on the heated grill and cook as desired.
Meanwhile, cut the bun in half, spread the two parts with a little softened butter and browned them in a nonstick skillet.
Put the base of the bun on a cutting board, add the spumiglia leaves, the Bûche de chèvre, the fig wedges, the patty, a pinch of the onion sauté and the Speck. Spread the other half with rosemary sauce and cover the bun. Pin everything together with a cocktail stick.

serve with
PALE LAGER BEER

veggyburger

difficulty	patty	season	inspiration	condiment
MEDIUM	VEGETABLE	4 SEASONS	ITALY	BASIL MAYONNAISE

1	bun
3 slices	Sorrento Scamorza cheese (20 g each)
100 g	eggplant
100 g	zucchini
3	meadow mushrooms
1	Sorrento beefsteak tomato
1 clove	garlic
30 g	basil mayonnaise
	thyme
	butter
	extra-virgin olive oil
	salt
	pepper

Make the basil mayonnaise (see "Sauces").
Cut the eggplant and zucchini into double slices and the mushrooms in half. Grill the vegetables and season them with a little oil, garlic, salt, coarsely milled pepper and thyme.
On a work surface put the first slice of Scamorza and cover with a slice of each vegetable on the grill. Repeat three times, creating a millefeuille of vegetables.
Place the millefeuille on the smooth hotplate and cover with the lid to melt the cheese.
Meanwhile, cut the bun in half, spread the two cut sides with butter, and brown in a nonstick skillet.
Put the base of the bun on a cutting board, spread it with a little basil mayonnaise and add the vegetable and tomato millefeuille. Spread the other half of the bun with basil mayonnaise and cover the burger. Pin everything together with a cocktail stick.

serve with
ARTISANAL CHINOTTO

hugeburger

difficulty	patty	season	inspiration	condiment
MEDIUM	TUNA	SPRING / SUMMER	ITALY	CAPER MAYONNAISE

1	**bun**
6	**black olives**
1	**fresh fennel**
1	**fresh spring onion**
30 g	**caper mayonnaise**
	parsley
	butter

Prepare the caper mayonnaise (see "Sauces").
Cut the tuna flesh into cubes and chop small with a
heavy knife, then mix with a trickle of oil and orange
zest; finally add the ground fennel seeds, bread-
crumbs and salt flakes.

	tuna patty
180 g	**fresh tuna flesh**
a few	**fennel seeds**
1	**orange**
1 handful	**breadcrumbs**
	extra-virgin olive oil
	salt flakes

Grease a round pastry ring 12 cm in diameter and
use it to shape the patty, smoothing the mixture
carefully and pressing it slightly.
Cook the patty in a skillet or on a smooth hotplate
with a little oil, initially with the steel pastry ring
to keep its shape, then using a spatula to brown it
nicely on both sides, cooking as desired.
Meanwhile, prepare a salad with the fennel cut into
julienne strips, the chopped black olives, the parsley,
the spring onion in thin slices and the orange peeled
to the quick and cut into chunks. Season with a
trickle of oil and a little salt.
Cut the bun in half, spread butter on the cut sides
and brown in a skillet.
Put the base of the bun on a cutting board, add a
little caper mayonnaise, then the patty and the fen-
nel salad prepared beforehand. Spread the other
half of the bun with caper mayonnaise and cover
the burger.

serve with
AMBER ALE

cultburger

difficulty
MEDIUM

patty
SCOTTONA BEEF

season
SPRING

inspiration
ITALY

condiment
GREEN PEPPER AND
JUNIPER MAYONNAISE

1	bun
1	Scottona beef patty 180 g
40 g	Taleggio
80 g	young spinach
2 leaves	red and green gentilina lettuce
1	whole leek
10 g	roasted hazelnuts
40 g	green pepper and juniper mayonnaise
1	nutmeg
1 clove	garlic
	butter
	extra-virgin olive oil
	fine salt

Prepare the mayonnaise with green pepper and juniper (see "Sauces").

Julienne the white of the leek and keep it in water with ice. In a skillet heat the oil and cook the garlic, removing it when it browns. Add the spinach, sautéing it rapidly to wilt it. Add salt to taste and spice it with a pinch of nutmeg.

Toast the hazelnuts and chop coarsely.

Oil the patty lightly and cook it on the heated grill as desired. Meanwhile, cut the bun in half, spread a little softened butter on it and brown the two halves in a pan.

Put the base of the bun on a cutting board, spread it with the mayonnaise, add the gentilina lettuce leaves, the patty, the Taleggio, the spinach, the julienned leek and the hazelnuts. Lastly spread the rest of the mayonnaise on the other half of the bun. Cover the burger and pin everything together with a cocktail stick.

special guest
GENTILINA LETTUCE

A traditional vegetable that has its roots in ancient Greece, gentilina lettuce has a delicate but attractive flavor and is an incredible source of minerals and vitamins. A simple but very versatile vegetable in the kitchen because it is always good, whether fresh, boiled or grilled.

serve with
PALE LAGER BEER

spicyburger

difficulty	patty	season	inspiration	condiment
MEDIUM	PORK	SPRING / SUMMER	BRITAIN	SPICY KETCHUP SAUCE

1	**bun**
1	**180 g pork burger**
1 sprig	**wild arugula (rocket)**
20 g	**medium Leicester cheese**
3 slices	**bacon**
1	**green chili**
25 g	**yogurt**
25 g	**mayonnaise**
50 g	**pineapple**
	coriander seeds
	curry powder
	ginger
	spicy ketchup sauce
	butter
	extra-virgin olive oil

Prepare the spiced pineapple, dicing it and putting the cubes in a bowl with the chopped coriander seeds, grated ginger, green chili cut into strips, the yogurt and the mayonnaise in a paste with the curry powder, and gently mix all the ingredients.
Trim and wash the wild arugula.
There are two ways to prepare the bacon. Either arrange the slices on a pan lined with baking paper and cook under the grill to the point desired, or put them in a skillet without oil or butter, so their fat melts making them crispy and flavorful.
Oil the patty lightly and cook it to perfection on the grill. Cover the patty with flakes of Leicester cheese and cover with the lid so it melts slightly.
Meanwhile, cut the bun in half and spread both cut sides with softened butter, then brown in a nonstick skillet.
Put the base of the bun on a cutting board and spread it with the spicy ketchup, then add the patty, arugula, spiced pineapple and crispy bacon.
Spread the other half of the bun with spicy ketchup and cover the bun. Pin everything together with a cocktail stick.

special guest
LEICESTER CHEESE

A dark red cheese, made with cow's milk, pressed and matured from 3 to 12 months. It comes from England and its birth in the county that gives it its name dates from the seventh century.

 serve with
RED BEER

upperburger

difficulty	patty	season	inspiration	condiment
MEDIUM	SHRIMP	SPRING / SUMMER	ITALY / AFRICA	CURRY SAUCE

1   **bun**
1   **zucchini**
1 leaf   **iceberg lettuce**
1   **lemon**
1 clove   **garlic**
30 g   **curry sauce**
   butter
   extra-virgin olive oil
   salt

   shrimp patty
150 g   **peeled shrimps**
50 g   **potatoes**
   fresh coriander
   double salt
   black pepper

Prepare the curry sauce (see "Sauces").
Spread a layer of double salt on an oven tray. Wash the potatoes and place them on the tray and cook in the oven at 180°C for about 1 hour. Once cooked (test using a toothpick), allow them to cool and then peel them.
To make the carpaccio of the zucchini cut them into ribbons, blanch them in a hot skillet and season with olive oil, garlic, salt and lemon zest.
On a cutting board coarsely chop the shrimps with a knife, add the freshly chopped coriander, adjust for the salt and black pepper crushed coarsely.
In a bowl, mix the chopped shrimp with the coarsely chopped potato.
Using a slightly greased round pastry cutter 12 cm in diameter, shape the patty and cook it on a smooth griddle. Allow two or three minutes per side for it to cook till rosy.
Cut the bun in half, spread the two slices with a little softened butter and brown them in a nonstick skillet.
Put the base of the bun on a cutting board, spread it with the curry sauce, add a sprig of julienned iceberg lettuce, then add the patty and the carpaccio of zucchini. Spread the other half of the bun with curry sauce and cover the burger.

serve with
TRAMINER AROMATIC WHITE WINE

earlyburger

difficulty
MEDIUM

patty
SCOTTONA BEEF

season
SUMMER

inspiration
FRANCE

condiment
OLD-STYLE MUSTARD
MAYONNAISE

1	**bun**
1	**Scottona beef patty 180 g**
1 slice	**Sorrento beefsteak tomato**
40 g	**Bûche de chèvre**
	(French cheese)
2 thin slices	**Prosciutto Crudo di Parma**
	Doppia Corona 18 months
2–3 rings	**red onion**
2 leaves	**red gentilina lettuce**
30 g	**old-style mustard mayonnaise**
2–3 flakes	**black summer truffle**
	mellow white grappa
	butter
	extra-virgin olive oil

Prepare the old-style mustard mayonnaise (see "Sauces").
Brush the patty lightly with oil and cook on the heated grill as desired.
Cut the bun in half, spread the two cut sides with a little softened butter, then brown in a nonstick skillet.
When done, put the base of the bun on a cutting board, spread with some mayonnaise, add the patty, the Bûche de chèvre, a little grated truffle, Prosciutto and spray with grappa. Finally add the gentilina leaves, tomato and the onion rings. Spread the other half of the bun with mustard mayonnaise and close the burger, securing it with a cocktail stick.

special guest
BÛCHE DE CHÈVRE

A pure goat's cheese from France, with a creamy paste, sweet outside, firm and savory inside. Even the rind can be eaten and is very tasty. Definitely sublime on bread, this goes great with artisanal buns.

serve with
RED BEER

13
feelburger

difficulty
HIGH

patty
SCOTTONA BEEF

season
SUMMER

inspiration
FUSION

condiment
GREEN TOMATO
CHUTNEY

1	**bun**
1	**Scottona beef patty 180 g**
2 slices	**Cheddar cheese**
1 slice	**artisanal smoked roasted ham**
2 slices	**pineapple**
2 leaves	**radicchio**
10 g	**green tomato chutney**
	dark rum
	butter
	extra-virgin olive oil
	pink pepper

Make the green tomato chutney (see "Sauces").
Lightly brush the patty with the oil and cook it on the heated grill as desired.
Place two slices of Cheddar on the patty and heat in a covered pan to melt them. Grill the two slices of pineapple and sprinkle with pink pepper.
Meanwhile, cut the bun in half, spread softened butter over the cut sides and brown in a nonstick skillet.
Spread a little chutney on the bottom half of the bun, then add the patty and spray with rum using an atomizer. Then add the ham, pineapple and the radicchio julienned. Spread the other half of the bun with green tomato chutney and pin everything together with a cocktail stick.

serve with
PALE WEIZEN BEER

easyburger

difficulty
EASY

patty
PORK

season
AUTUMN

inspiration
ITALY / NORTH AMERICA

condiment
BARBECUE SAUCE

1	**bun**
1	**180 g pork patty**
2 slices	**Sorrento smoked Scamorza cheese**
1 slice	**Sorrento beefsteak tomato**
1 leaf	**lettuce**
2–3 rings	**red onion**
30 g	**barbecue sauce**
	butter
	extra-virgin olive oil

Brush the patty lightly with oil and place on the heated grill till done.

Put the Scamorza on the patty and cover with the lid just long enough to melt it.

Meanwhile, cut the bun in half, spread the two slices with softened butter and brown in a nonstick skillet. Place the bottom half of the bun on a cutting board and add the lettuce, patty, tomato and onion rings. Spread the other half of the bread warm with plenty of barbecue sauce and cover the bun. Use a cocktail stick to pin everything together.

special guest
SORRENTO SMOKED SCAMORZA

A typical product of Campania with a markedly smoky taste, pleasant fresh or cooked. It has been documented for many centuries and has appeared on the shepherds' stalls in Neapolitan nativity scenes since the early 17th century.

serve with
PALE LAGER BEER

peakburger

difficulty
MEDIUM

patty
SCOTTONA BEEF

season
SPRING

inspiration
ITALY / FRANCIA

condiment
OLD-STYLE MUSTARD
MAYONNAISE

1	**bun**
1	**Scottona beef patty 180 g**
1	**Jerusalem artichoke**
1 sprig	**wild arugula**
1 slice	**artisanal smoked roasted ham**
30 g	**Parmigiano Reggiano 24 months**
30 g	**old-style mustard mayonnaise**
	butter
	peanut oil
	extra-virgin olive oil
	black pepper

Prepare the mustard mayonnaise (see "Sauces"). Peel the Jerusalem artichoke and cut into thin slices, like potato chips ("crisps") and fry it in peanut oil. Wash and clean the arugula.

Brush the patty lightly with oil, put it on the heated grill and cook as desired.

Meanwhile, cut the bun in half, spread the cut sides with a little softened butter and brown in a pan.

Put the base of the bun on a cutting board, spread with a little mustard mayonnaise, add the patty, arugula, ham, the shavings of Parmigiano, the Jerusalem artichoke chips and black pepper. Spread the other half of the bun with the rest of the mayonnaise and cover the burger. Pin together with a cocktail stick.

☆ special guest
JERUSALEM ARTICHOKE

Also known as a "German turnip", this plant was eaten long ago for its edible root, then was gradually supplanted by the potato, which is cooked in a similar way. The tubers of the Jerusalem artichoke are highly nutritious and can be eaten raw or cooked.

serve with
PILSNER BEER

heartburger

difficulty	patty	season	inspiration	condiment
MEDIUM	SCOTTONA BEEF	AUTUMN	NORTH AMERICA	PEANUT SAUCE

1	**bun**
1	**Scottona beef patty 180 g**
1 slice	**artisanal smoked roasted ham**
30 g	**Parmigiano Reggiano 24 months**
50 g	**fresh oyster mushrooms**
2 leaves	**radicchio**
30 g	**peanut sauce**
1 clove	**garlic**
	butter
	extra-virgin olive oil
	fine salt
	black peppercorns

Prepare the peanut sauce (see "Sauces").
Brush and clean the oyster mushrooms and cut them into slices. Meanwhile, in a skillet, heat a little extra-virgin olive oil and soften the garlic in it, then remove and sauté the oyster mushrooms in the oil for a minute, adjust for salt and pepper in coarsely crushed grains and keep everything warm.
Brush the patty with a little extra-virgin olive oil, put it on the heated grill and cook as desired.
Meanwhile, cut the bun in half, pour a drizzle of softened butter on the cut sides and brown in a skillet.
Put the base of the bun on a cutting board and then add the radicchio julienned, the patty, ham, mushrooms and Parmigiano shavings. Spread the other half of the bun with peanut sauce. Now cover the patty and pin everything together with a cocktail stick.

special guests
OYSTER MUSHROOMS AND PEANUT SAUCE

Oyster mushrooms are typical of Southern Italy.
Crunchy, they contrast with the peanut sauce, and make
for a taste trip between Italy and America.

serve with
PALE LAGER BEER

A recipe always has the same ingredients except one, your mindset. Because it changes every time, depending on the person you want to make it for.

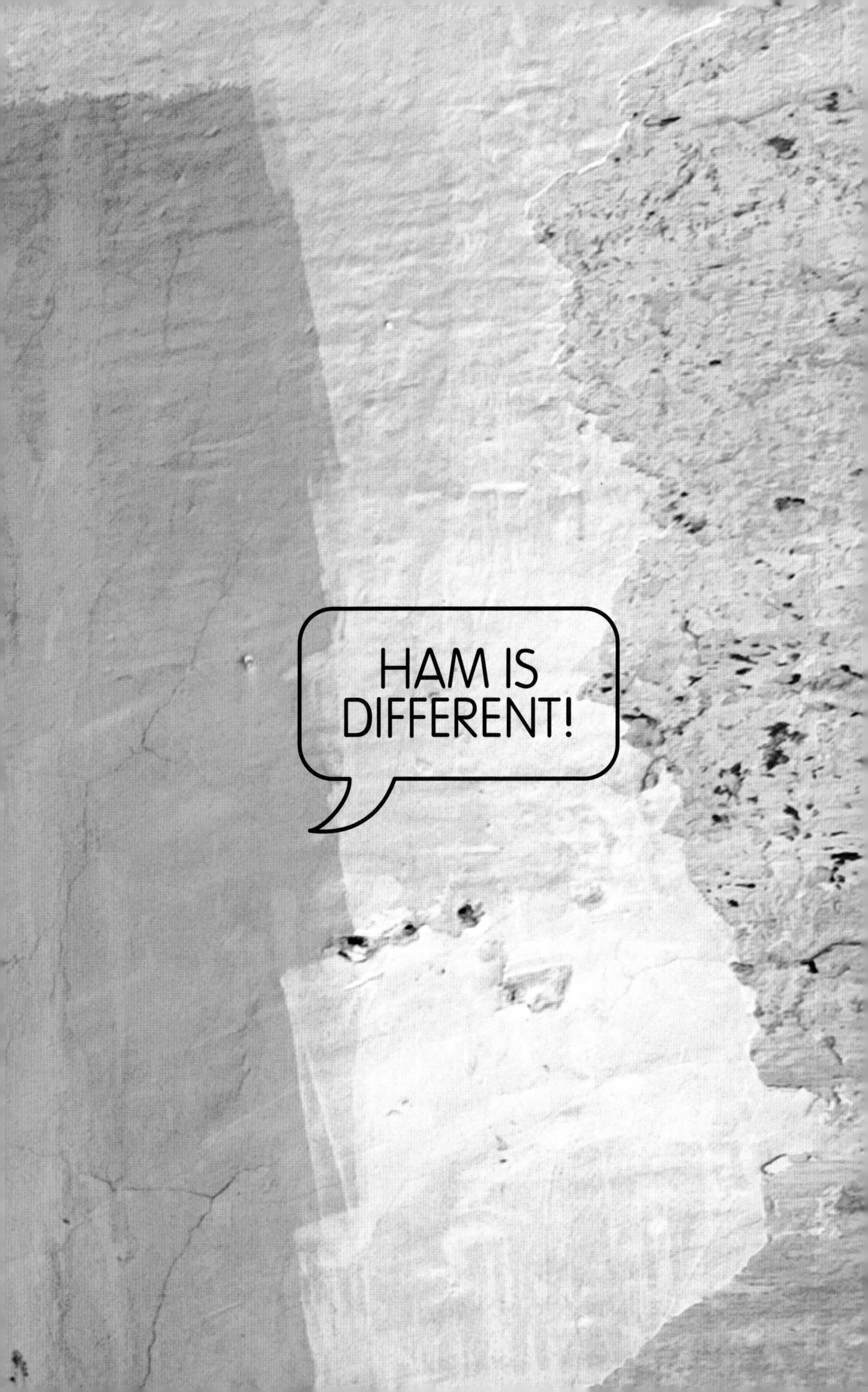
HAM IS DIFFERENT!

soulburger

difficulty	patty	season	inspiration	condiment
MEDIUM	SCOTTONA BEEF	4 SEASONS	NORTH AMERICA BRITAIN	BARBECUE SAUCE RELISH SAUCE

1	**bun**
1	**Scottona beef patty 180 g**
2 slices	**Cheddar cheese**
3 slices	**bacon**
1	**egg**
1 slice	**Sorrento beefsteak tomato**
1 leaf	**lettuce**
3 slices	**cucumber**
2–3 rings	**red onion**
30 g	**barbecue sauce**
20 g	**relish sauce**
	butter
	extra-virgin olive oil
	fine salt

You can prepare the crispy bacon either by arranging the slices on a plate lined with oven paper and roast under the grill as desired, or roast them in a skillet without oil or butter; the bacon fat will melt and make the bacon crispy and flavorful.

Brush the patty with a little oil and put it on the heated grill until it is cooked as desired.

Put the slices of Cheddar on the patty, cover with the lid and let it melt slightly.

Cut the bun in half, spread the two slices with a little softened butter and brown them in a nonstick skillet.

Meanwhile, prepare a fried egg and divide the yolk from the white: warn a little butter and extra-virgin olive oil in a pan, put a round pastry cutter over it and pour in first the egg white and then make a dimple in the center and add the yolk. Cook and season with salt to taste.

Put the base of the bun on a cutting board and add first the lettuce leaf, tomato, cucumber and onion, then the patty, the bacon and the egg and pour over the relish. Finally spread the other half of the bun with the barbecue sauce. Cover the burger and pin everything together with a cocktail stick.

special guest
RELISH SAUCE

A vegetarian seasoning, spicy, fruity and typically British. Based on fruit and sugar, it enhances the flavors of meat and fish.

serve with
INDIA PALE ALE

fusiontartar

difficulty
MEDIUM

tartare
SCOTTONA BEEF

season
SPRING / SUMMER

inspiration
SOUTH AMERICA / FUSION

condiment
TARTAR SAUCE

180 g	Scottona beef fillet
1	red bell pepper
1	yellow bell pepper
1	vine tomato
1	ripe avocado
1	red onion
1	lime
30 g	tartar sauce
	Worcestershire sauce
	extra-virgin olive oil
	fleur de sel
	black pepper

Prepare the meat carefully to make a tartar: slice it quite thin, then into strips, then chop it small with a knife. Drizzle with olive oil, add a pinch of pepper and a few drops of Worcestershire sauce, then mix it delicately.

Blanch the tomato, remove the skin, cut it in half and let it drain. When drained, dice it together with the onion, mix with the tomato and combine all with the tartar.

Now make the brunoise of bell peppers by dicing the strips of peppers. Then cut the avocado into chunks, sprinkle them with a little lime juice and dress them with fleur de sel and a drizzle of olive oil.

In the middle of a plate put a third of the tartar in a round pastry cutter, 10 cm in diameter, greased inside, press lightly and cover with half the avocado mixture. Add another third of tartar, the other half of the avocado and complete with the remaining tartar. Remove the pastry cutter and garnish with the brunoise of bell peppers.

Serve with a bowl of tartar sauce (see "Sauces").

special guest
TARTAR SAUCE

A dense white sauce based on mayonnaise.
Of French origin, it has now become
an international must with meat and fish.

serve with
TRAMINER AROMATIC WHITE WINE

sundayburger

difficulty
EASY

patty
SCOTTONA BEEF

season
SUMMER

inspiration
ITALY / CENTRAL AMERICA

condiment
MINT
YOGURT

1	**bun**
1	**Scottona beef patty 180 g**
1 sprig	**wild arugula**
40 g	**Parmigiano Reggiano 24 months**
1	**lime**
5 leaves	**fresh mint**
40 g	**Greek yogurt**
	light rum
	butter
	extra-virgin olive oil
	peppercorns

Cut the lime into thin slices.
Clean and wash the arugula carefully.
Mix the yogurt with a trickle of olive oil and two or three chopped mint leaves.
Brush the patty lightly with oil, then put it on the heated grill and cook as desired.
Meanwhile, cut the bun in half, spread the cut sides with softened butter and then brown them in a non-stick pan.
Now put the base of the bun on a cutting board and add the arugula with a drizzle of extra-virgin olive oil, the patty, the Parmigiano, lime and mint. Add the coarsely crushed pepper and spray with the light rum. Spread the other half of the bun with the minty yogurt and cover. Pin everything together with a cocktail stick.

serve with
INDIA PALE ALE

giftburger

difficulty
HIGH

patty
SCOTTONA BEEF

season
WINTER

inspiration
ITALY

condiment
WALNUT PESTO

1	**bun**
1	**Scottona beef patty 180 g**
2 slices	**Guanciale di Norcia (pork cheek from Norcia)**
30 g	**mustard mayonnaise**
15 g	**Tuscan Pecorino matured 12 months**
50 g	**fresh spinach**
15 g	**walnut pesto**
1 clove	**garlic**
	butter
	extra-virgin olive oil
	sea salt in flakes

Make the mustard mayonnaise (see "Sauces").
Clean the spinach, wash in several waters to remove any soil and sauté quickly in garlic and oil. Keep it warm.
Brush the patty lightly with oil, put it on the heated grill and cook as desired.
Cut the bun in half, spread the cut sides with a little softened butter and brown in a nonstick skillet.
Place the bottom half of the roll on a cutting board, spread with a little walnut pesto, put the patty on it, then the spinach flavored with a few flakes of salt, Pecorino and Guanciale. Spread the other half of the bun with mustard mayonnaise and close the burger. Pin everything together with a cocktail stick.

 special guest
GUANCIALE DI NORCIA (PORK CHEEK FROM NORCIA)

We chose this specialty, pork's cheek from Norcia, because its special curing in wood-burning chimneys for about 2 months makes it very tasty. The meat comes from large hogs, adults of the carefully selected white breed never subjected to any manipulation. Hence it is smoked and matured in quite natural ways.

serve with
RED BEER

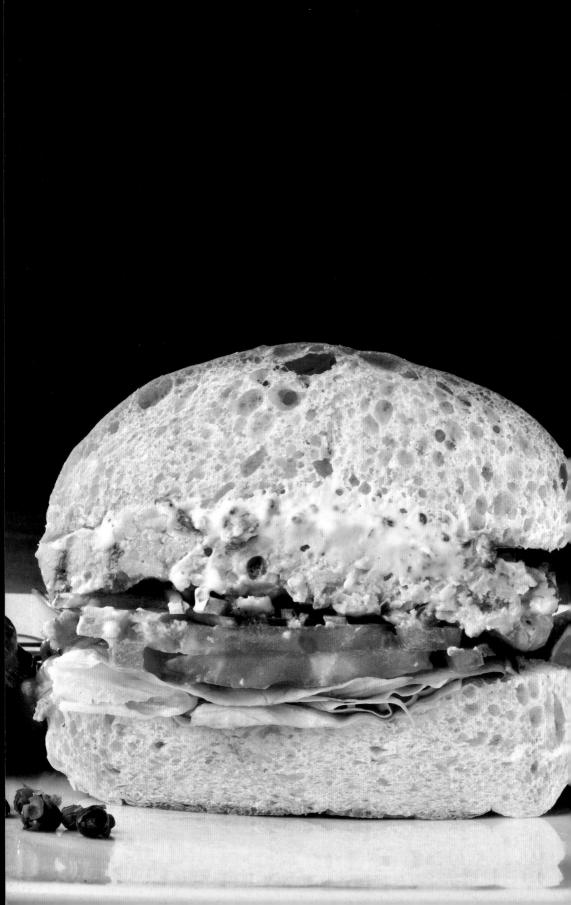

riseburger

difficulty
MEDIUM

patty
SALMON

season
SPRING / SUMMER

inspiration
FUSION

condiment
YOGURT AND MUSTARD
MAYONNAISE

1	**bun**
1 slice	**Sorrento beefsteak tomato**
1 leaf	**lettuce**
2-3 rings	**red onion**
20 g	**mayonnaise**
10 g	**yogurt**
1 teaspoonful	**mustard seeds**
	butter
	salmon patty
180 g	**fresh salmon flesh**
1	**green chili**
1	**lime**
	pink pepper
	extra-virgin olive oil
	fine salt

Prepare the sauce by mixing the mayonnaise, yogurt and mustard seeds.

Dice the flesh of the salmon, then chop the pieces smaller with a knife and add one green chili, some salt, pink pepper and a grating of lime zest.

Grease a round pastry cutter 12 cm in diameter and use it to shape the patty. Put it on a well heated hotplate and cook as desired.

Meanwhile, cut the bun in half spread the cut sides with butter and brown in a nonstick skillet.

Rest the base of the bun on a cutting board and add the lettuce, tomatoes, onion rings and patty. Spread the other half of the bun with plenty of yogurt and mustard mayonnaise and cover the burger. Pin everything together with a cocktail stick.

serve with
WEIZEN BEER

touchburger

difficulty	patty	season	inspiration	condiment
MEDIUM	SCOTTONA BEEF	WINTER	ITALY / NORTH AMERICA	BARBECUE SAUCE

1	**bun**
1	**Scottona beef patty 180 g**
1 slice	**artisanal smoked roasted ham**
30 g	**buffalo-milk Gorgonzola**
1 leaf	**gentilina or lollo lettuce**
60 g	**radicchio**
1 clove	**garlic**
1	**red onion**
15 g	**redcurrant glaze**
30 g	**barbecue sauce**
	mellow white grappa
	butter
	extra-virgin olive oil
	salt
	pepper

Prepare the redcurrant glaze (see "Sauces").

In a skillet heat the oil, fry the garlic lightly and remove it after a few minutes, then add the radicchio and red onion. Sweat them, then add the grappa and let it evaporate, add salt and pepper to taste and when braised keep it warm.

Brush the patty lightly with oil, put it on the heated grill and cook as desired, then brush with the redcurrant glaze.

Meanwhile, cut the bun in half, spread the cut sides with a little softened butter, and brown them in a skillet.

Put the base of the bun on a cutting board, add the lettuce, patty, Gorgonzola flakes, a spoonful of braised radicchio and the ham. Cover with the other half of the bun sprinkled with barbecue sauce. Use a cocktail stick to pin everything together.

special guest
BUFFALO-MILK GORGONZOLA

A typical Italian cheese, made from cow and buffalo milk, left to mature for a long period together. Its hard dark rind conceals a soft, flavorful cheese.

serve with
RED BEER

greenburger

difficulty	patty	season	inspiration	condiment
MEDIUM	VEGETABLES	SPRING / SUMMER	ITALY / GREECE	YOGURT SAUCE

1	bun
1	Sorrento beefsteak tomato
1 leaf	iceberg lettuce
1	spring onion
30 g	yogurt sauce
20 g	basil pesto
	thyme
	butter
	vegetarian patty
200 g	potatoes
100 g	zucchini
100 g	carrots
1 clove	garlic
3 leaves	basil
	extra-virgin olive oil
	double salt
	salt
	pepper

Prepare the yogurt sauce (see "Sauces") and the basil pesto to the classic recipe.

First prepare a vegetarian patty as follows: line a baking tray with a layer of double salt, place the previously washed potatoes in the oven and cook them at 180°C for about 1 hour. When they are done (check by pricking them with a toothpick), allow them to cool and then peel and dice into large pieces.

Dice the zucchini and carrots and julienne the spring onion. Heat a little olive oil and a clove of garlic in a skillet. Remove the garlic as soon as it browns. Add the zucchini and the basil and deglaze with a little water, making sure they remain crisp. Repeat this process with the carrots. Allow to cool. Put the potatoes and vegetables in a bowl with a pinch of salt and pepper, mix and shape the patties, using a greased pastry cutter 12 cm in diameter or a pastry mold as preferred.

Brush the patty lightly with oil and sear both sides in a very hot skillet.

Meanwhile, cut the bun in half and spread the two cut sides with a little softened butter, then brown them in a skillet.

Put the base of the bun on a cutting board and spread it with a little yogurt sauce. Now add the lettuce leaf julienned, the patty, the tomato, the julienned spring onion, a teaspoonful of basil pesto and flavor with a little thyme. Finally take the other half of the bun, spread it with sauce and cover the burger. Pin everything together with a cocktail stick.

serve with
GINGER BEER

24

landburger

difficulty	patty	season	inspiration	condiment
HIGH	SCOTTONA BEEF	SUMMER	FRANCE	HOLY SAUCE

Prepare the holy sauce (see "Sauces"). Slice the onion finely and dice the vegetables into regular pieces about 1 cm per side to make the ratatouille. Put all the ingredients in a large bowl, add salt, thyme, a few bay leaves, stir and put in a ready heated skillet containing 30 g extra-virgin olive oil and a trace of garlic. Cook for a minute, cover level with water and simmer for about 10 minutes.

Lightly brush the patty with extra-virgin olive oil and cook it on the heated grill as desired. Arrange the slices of Scamorza on the patty and melt in a covered pan.

Meanwhile, cut the bun in half, spread both sides with a little softened butter and brown them in a skillet.

Put the base of the bun on a cutting board, add the lettuce, ratatouille, patty, pitted olives, and dried tomatoes julienned. Spread the other half of the bun with the holy sauce and cover the burger. Use a cocktail stick to pin everything together.

1	bun
1	Scottona beef patty 180 g
1 leaf	lettuce
5–6	pitted black olives
2 pieces	dried tomatoes in oil
1 slice	Sorrento Scamorza cheese
40 g	holy sauce
	butter
	extra-virgin olive oil
	ratatouille
1	zucchini
½	bell pepper
1	eggplant
1	tomato
1	potato
1	onion
1 clove	garlic
	thyme
	bay leaves
30 g	extra-virgin olive oil
	fine salt

special guest
RATATOUILLE

Ratatouille is a traditional Provencal dish of frugal peasant origin. It is very summery, being made with fresh vegetables. This is a special version that deviates slightly from the original.

serve with
AMBER ALE

slightburger

difficulty
MEDIUM

patty
CHICKEN

season
SPRING

inspiration
ITALY

condiment
CARROT AND CUMIN
MAYONNAISE

1	**bun**
1	**chicken patty 180 g**
1 slice	**Emmentaler AOC matured in caves**
3 slices	**tomatoes**
1 sprig	**wild arugula**
30 g	**carrot and cumin mayonnaise**
	butter
	extra-virgin olive oil

Make the carrot and cumin mayonnaise (see "Sauces"). Brush the patty lightly with oil and put it on the heated grill until well done.

Put the Emmentaler on the patty and cover with the lid for a few seconds so it melts.

Meanwhile, cut the bun in half, spread the two cut sides with a little softened butter and brown them in a nonstick skillet.

Put the base of the bun on a cutting board, spread it with a little mayonnaise, add the arugula, the tomatoes and the patty. Spread the other half with plenty of carrot and cumin mayonnaise and cover the burger. Pin everything together with a cocktail stick.

special guest
EMMENTALER AOC MATURED IN CAVES

Considered the king of cheeses, it has a full, vigorous flavor imparted by aging for 12 months in the caves of the valley of the River Emme, in Canton Bern, Switzerland, hence its name.

serve with
AMBER ALE

holyxmasburger

difficulty	patty	season	inspiration	condiment
MEDIUM	SCOTTONA BEEF	WINTER	ITALY	ROSEMARY SAUCE

1	bun
1	Scottona beef patty 180 g
2 leaves	radicchio
30 g	rosemary sauce
	butter
	extra-virgin olive oil

	autumn sauté
40 g	chestnuts
30 g	porcini mushrooms
30 g	meadow mushrooms
30 g	Melannurca
2 slices	bacon
1 leaf	sage
1 thin slice	white onion
	mellow white grappa
	extra-virgin olive oil
	salt
	pepper

There are two ways of preparing the bacon. Either arrange the slices on a pan lined with baking paper and cook under the grill to the point desired, or put them in a skillet without oil or butter, so their fat melts making them crispy and flavorful.

Prepare the rosemary sauce (see "Sauces").

For the sauté: warm the oil in a pan, add the bacon cut into julienne strips, onion, sage, chestnuts, porcini and meadow mushrooms sliced. Add the Melannurca thinly sliced, then cook for a few minutes and deglaze the mixture with a dash of grappa. Season with salt and pepper, and keep the sauté warm.

Lightly brush the patty with oil and cook it on the heated grill till cooked as desired.

Cut the bun in half, spread both cut sides with a little softened butter, and brown in a nonstick skillet.

Put the base of the bun on a cutting board, spread with a little cheese sauce with rosemary, add the radicchio julienned, the patty, crispy bacon and hot sauté. Spread the other half of the bun with the remaining sauce, cover the burger and pin everything together with a cocktail stick.

☆ special guest
MELANNURCA

A small, very ancient apple: pictures of it have been found in the excavations of Herculaneum. It is typical of Campania and is called the Queen of Apples for its noble, distinctive, tart flavor. Unique among Mediterranean fruit, and excellent with meat.

serve with
RED WINE PUNCH WITH CINNAMON AND CLOVE

kidburger

difficulty
EASY

patty
SCOTTONA BEEF

season
4 SEASONS

inspiration
NORTH AMERICA

condiment
MAYONNAISE AND KETCHUP

1	**bun**
1	**Scottona beef patty 180 g**
2 slices	**Cheddar cheese**
	stick chips
15 g	**mayonnaise**
15 g	**ketchup**
	butter
	extra-virgin olive oil

Prepare stick chips made to the recipe (see "Fries") and keep them warm.
Brush the patty lightly with extra-virgin olive oil, put it on the heated grill and cook as desired. Arrange the slices of Cheddar on the patty and cover with the lid till the cheese melts. Meanwhile, cut the bun in half, spread a little melted butter on both sides and brown it in a nonstick skillet.
Put the base of the bun on a cutting board, place the patty on it with some of the fries and season with ketchup and mayonnaise. Then cover everything with the other half of the bun and pin together with a cocktail stick.

serve with
HAND MADE LEMONADE

whiteburger

difficulty
MEDIUM

patty
chicken

season
4 SEASONS

inspiration
ITALY

condiment
CURRY SAUCE

1	**bun**
1	**chicken patty 180 g**
1 slice	**artisanal smoked roasted ham**
1 slice	**Sorrento smoked Scamorza cheese**
1 slice	**Sorrento beefsteak tomato**
1 leaf	**lettuce**
2–3 rings	**onion**
30 g	**curry sauce**
	butter
	extra-virgin olive oil

Prepare the curry sauce (see "Sauces").
Brush the patty lightly with oil, put it on the heated grill and cook it till it is done.
Put the smoked cheese on the patty and cover with the lid for a few seconds until it melts.
Turn off the heat and place the ham on the grill for a few minutes.
Cut the bun in half, spread the cut sides with a little softened butter and brown them in a nonstick skillet.
Put the base of the bun on a cutting board and add the lettuce, patty, tomato, ham and onion rings. Spread the other half of the bun with plenty of curry sauce and cover the burger. Pin everything together with a cocktail stick.

serve with
TRAMINER AROMATIC WHITE WINE

smartburger

difficulty
MEDIUM

patty
SCOTTONA BEEF

season
SPRING / SUMMER

inspiration
JAPAN / SOUTH AMERICA

condiments
WASABI SAUCE

1	**bun**
1	**Scottona beef patty 180 g**
2 slices	**artisanal smoked roasted ham**
1	**Sorrento beefsteak tomato**
1 sprig	**wild arugula**
2 slices	**mango**
2–3 rings	**red onion**
30 g	**mayonnaise**
	wasabi
	butter
	extra-virgin olive oil
	Himalayan pink salt
	pink peppercorn

Mix the mayonnaise with a dab of wasabi dissolved in a teaspoonful of water.
Clean and carefully wash the wild arugula.
Brush the patty lightly and put it on the heated grill until cooked as desired.
Meanwhile, cut the bun in half, spread the two cut sides with a little softened butter, and brown them in a skillet.
Put the base of the bun on a cutting board, then add the ham, arugula, the mango sprinkled with pink pepper, the tomato, the patty and finally the onion rings. Spread the other half of the bread with the wasabi mayonnaise. Cover the burger and pin everything together with a cocktail stick.

serve with
PALE WEIZEN BEER

blackburger

difficulty	patty	season	inspiration	condiment
EASY	SCOTTONA BEEF	WINTER	ITALY / NORTH AMERICA	BARBECUE SAUCE

1	bun
1	Scottona beef patty 180 g
50 g	fresh meadow mushrooms
40 g	Provolone Auricchio Stravecchio Scorzanera cheese
3 slices	bacon
1 leaf	lettuce
40 g	barbecue sauce
1	lemon
	butter
	extra-virgin olive oil
	fine salt
	milled pepper

Brush and clean the mushrooms carefully, slice thinly and season with a little olive oil, salt, pepper and a dash of lemon.

Put a little oil on the patty, set it on the heated grill and cook as desired. Meanwhile, prepare the crispy bacon to the recipe.

Cut the bun in half, spread a little softened butter on the cut sides and cook the two halves golden brown in a nonstick skillet.

Rest the base of the bun on a cutting board and add the lettuce leaf, patty, thinly sliced mushrooms, slivers of Auricchio, crispy bacon and finally pour a little barbecue sauce in the middle. Finally spread the other half of the bun with the rest of the sauce and cover the burger. Pin everything together with a cocktail stick.

special guest
PROVOLONE AURICCHIO STRAVECCHIO SCORZANERA

An inimitable Italian excellence, representing the ancient art of cheese making, matured for more than a year in special buildings.

serve with
PORTER BEER

legendburger

difficulty	patty	season	inspiration	condiment
EASY	SCOTTONA BEEF	SUMMER	ITALY	BASIL MAYONNAISE

1	**bun**
1	**Scottona beef patty 180 g**
1 slice	**smoked Provola cheese made from fresh buffalo milk**
1 slice	**Sorrento beefsteak tomato**
1	**eggplant**
1	**zucchini**
1	**bell pepper**
30 g	**basil mayonnaise**
1 clove	**garlic**
	fresh thyme
	butter
	extra-virgin olive oil
	salt

Prepare the basil mayonnaise (see "Sauces").
Wash the bell pepper and roast it whole on the grill, turning it from time to time so it roasts all over. Once well done, put it in an airtight container until it cools, then peel it, remove the seeds and cut into strips.
Cut the eggplant and zucchini into thin long slices and roast them on the grill. Mix all the roasted vegetables and season with olive oil, salt and thyme and squeeze the juice from a clove of garlic over them. Store them in a cool place.
Heat the grill and roast the patty lightly brushed with oil. When cooked as desired put a slice of Provola on the patty and cover for a few seconds to melt it.
Meanwhile, cut the bun in half, spread the two cut sides with a little softened butter and let them brown in a nonstick skillet.
Spread the base of the bun with the basil mayonnaise and put it on a cutting board. Add the patty, tomato and grilled vegetables. Spread the other half of the bread with the rest of the mayonnaise. Cover and pin all the ingredients together with a cocktail stick.

serve with
LAGER BEER

freeburger

difficulty
EASY

patty
SEITAN

season
SPRING / SUMMER

inspiration
ITALY

condiment
BASIL MAYONNAISE

1	**bun**
1	**seitan patty**
1 slice	**Sorrento beefsteak tomato**
1 leaf	**lettuce**
1	**eggplant**
30 g	**basil mayonnaise**
	butter
	extra-virgin olive oil
	salt

Prepare the basil mayonnaise (see "Sauces").
Cut the eggplant into slices, grill them and season with salt and oil.
Put the patty in a well heated nonstick skillet until done.
Meanwhile cut the bun in two, spread the cut sides with a little softened butter and brown them in a skillet.
To assemble the burger, place the base of the bun on a cutting board and spread with basil mayonnaise. Add the ingredients as follows: lettuce, tomato, seitan patty and grilled eggplant. Spread the other half of the bread with basil mayonnaise and cover the burger. Pin everything together with a cocktail stick.

☆ special guest
SEITAN

A high-protein foodstuff from China, made from gluten from soft wheat, barley or Khorasan wheat. An alternative for those who love a vegetarian diet.

serve with
WEIZEN BEER

jewelburger

difficulty	patty	season	inspiration	condiment
MEDIUM	LOBSTER	SPRING / SUMMER	SPAIN	CITRUS MAYONNAISE

1	**bun**
50 g	**red bell peppers**
50 g	**cherry tomatoes**
1	**orange**
1	**lemon**
1 sprig	**wild arugula**
30 g	**citrus mayonnaise**
	butter
	extra-virgin olive oil
	double salt
	fine salt
	lobster patty
500 g	**lobster**
50 g	**potatoes**
20 g	**chives**
	orange zest
	salt

Prepare some Catalan-style diced vegetables with red bell peppers, chives and tomatoes, then season lightly with olive oil, salt and a dash of orange and lemon juice.

Make the citrus mayonnaise (see "Sauces").

Spread on a baking tray a layer of double salt and place the potatoes previously washed on it. Roast in the oven at 180°C for about 1 hour. Once cooked (check the potatoes by sticking a toothpick Into them) allow them to cool and peel.

Immerse the lobster in a pan of boiling water for a maximum of ten minutes, cool and then remove the meat from the claws and the rest of the body and cut into small pieces. Mix the pieces of lobster gently with the orange zest, chopped chives, mashed potato and salt. Shape using a round greased pastry cutter 12 cm in diameter. Smooth the mixture carefully and press lightly.

Trickle a little oil on a smooth hotplate and cook the patty. At first leave the pastry cutter to keep the form intact. Brown on both sides, 2 or 3 minutes per side, using a spatula to turn the patty.

Cut the bun in half and spread the cut sides with a little softened butter, then brown them in a nonstick skillet.

Put the base of the bun on a cutting board and spread it with the citrus mayonnaise, then add a sprig of arugula, the patty and a spoonful of diced vegetables. Spread the other half of the bun with mayonnaise and close the burger.

serve with
PROSECCO SPARKLING WHITE WINE

FEEL GOOD

How much do authentic feelings,
simple gestures and small pleasures
mean to you? You will discover this whenever
you make a holy burger.

risingburger

difficulty
MEDIUM

patty
SCOTTONA BEEF

season
WINTER

inspiration
FUSION

condiment
BALSAMIC VINEGAR
KETCHUP

1	**bun**
1	**Scottona beef patty 180 g**
30 g	**Feta cheese**
1 leaf	**lettuce**
1 pinch	**oregano**
30 g	**balsamic vinegar ketchup**
	butter
	extra-virgin olive oil

creamed eggplant

1	**eggplant**
1 clove	**garlic**
1 sprig	**basil**
a few seeds	**cumin**
	extra-virgin olive oil
	fine salt

Prick the eggplant with the point of a knife and roast for 15 minutes in the oven heated to 180°C, then let it cool. Once it is soft, remove the pulp with a spoon and chop it, using a heavy knife, on a cutting board with olive oil, garlic, basil, salt and a few cumin seeds. Keep it in a cool place.
Brush the patty lightly with oil and roast it on the heated grill as desired.
Meanwhile, cut the bun in half, spread the cut sides with a little softened butter and brown them quickly in a nonstick skillet.
Put the base of the bun on a cutting board and add the filling: first the patty, then the eggplant pesto, the Feta cheese crumbled and the lettuce leaf on top. Spread the other half of the patty with balsamic vinegar ketchup and oregano. Cover and pin together with a cocktail stick.

serve with
AMBER ALE

skillburger

difficulty
MEDIUM

patty
SCOTTONA BEEF

season
WINTER

inspiration
ITALY

condiment
TRUFFLE MAYONNAISE

1	**bun**
1	**Scottona beef patty 180 g**
2 slices	**Prosciutto Crudo di Parma**
	18 months Doppia Corona
20 g	**Parmigiano Reggiano 24 months**
1 handful	**freshly cut spinach**
2	**fresh meadow mushrooms**
30 g	**mayonnaise**
	black truffle paste
	butter
	extra-virgin olive oil
	salt
	black pepper

In a bowl mix the mayonnaise with a teaspoonful of black truffle paste to make truffle mayonnaise.
Brush the mushrooms, wipe them dry and cut them into thin slices. Season them with a little olive oil, salt and pepper.
Wash the spinach carefully.
Brush the patty with a little oil and cook on the heated grill as desired.
Meanwhile, cut the bun in half, spread both cut sides with a little softened butter, and brown them in a nonstick skillet.
Put the base of the bun on a cutting board, add the spinach seasoned with olive oil and salt, the Parmigiano, Prosciutto, the carpaccio of mushrooms with seasoning and the patty. Spread the other half of the bread with the truffle mayonnaise and cover the burger. Pin everything together with a cocktail stick.

serve with
MORELLINO RED WINE

faithburger

difficulty
EASY

patty
SCOTTONA BEEF

season
4 SEASONS

inspiration
ITALY

condiment
BARBECUE SAUCE

1	**bun**
1	**Scottona beef patty 180 g**
30 g	**Calabrian 'Nduja**
2 slices	**Sorrento smoked Scamorza cheese**
1 slice	**Sorrento beefsteak tomato**
3–4 rings	**red onion**
1 leaf	**iceberg lettuce**
30 g	**barbecue sauce**
	butter
	extra-virgin olive oil

Lightly brush the patty with oil, place it on the heated grill and cook as desired.

Put the slices of Scamorza on top of the patty, and cover with the lid until the cheese begins to melt.

Meanwhile, cut the bun in half, spread a little softened butter over the cut sides and brown the two halves in a nonstick skillet.

Put the base of the bun on a cutting board and place on it the lettuce, the tomato, the onion, the patty, and top with the 'Nduja. Spread the other half of the bun with the barbecue sauce and cover the bun. Pin everything together with a cocktail stick.

 special guest
CALABRIAN 'NDUJA

'Nduja is a typical smoked fancy meat from Calabria, made with scraps of pork, above all the fatty parts, and with the addition of Calabrian hot chili. Its popularity has made it a common ingredient in the gourmet kitchen.

serve with
PALE LAGER BEER

soundburger

difficulty	patty	season	inspiration	condiment
MEDIUM	SCOTTONA BEEF	SUMMER	ITALY / FUSION	HOLY SAUCE

Prepare the holy sauce (see "Sauces").

For the tapenade put the black olives on a cutting board and chop them with a knife, gradually adding the capers, garlic, parsley, lime peel and olive oil. To make sesame salt, lightly brown the sesame seeds over low heat in a nonstick skillet, stirring circularly with a wooden spoon. They will be done to perfection when the seeds start popping. Then combine the salt with the seeds either by crushing them or whizzing them in the blender to a slightly oily powder.

Heat the grill, wash the peppers, dry them, roast them well on all sides, and then put them in an airtight container to cool. Peel them, cut them open, remove the seeds and pith, and cut them into strips. Season with the olive oil, garlic, lime zest, basil and sesame salt previously prepared.

Mix the Caprino with a little pepper, a dash of olive oil, the chopped parsley and a trickle of water.

Brush the patty lightly with oil and cook it on the heated grill as desired.

Cut the bun in half, spread a little softened butter on the cut sides and brown them in a skillet.

Put the base of the bun on a cutting board and add the iceberg lettuce julienned, the patty, the peppers, the Caprino mousse and the black olive tapenade. Spread the other half of the bun with the holy sauce and cover the burger. Pin everything together with a cocktail stick.

1	**bun**
1	**Scottona beef patty 180 g**
50 g	**Caprino cheese**
1	**red bell pepper**
1	**yellow bell pepper**
2 leaves	**iceberg lettuce**
2 leaves	**basil**
1 clove	**garlic**
30 g	**holy sauce**
	lime zest
	butter
	extra-virgin olive oil
	pink peppercorn

	tapenade
10	**pitted black olives**
3	**capers**
1 clove	**garlic**
1 sprig	**parsley**
	lime zest
	extra-virgin olive oil

	sesame salt
60 g	**sesame seeds**
60 g	**fine salt**

special guest
SESAME SALT

An original creation, inspired by gomasio, a classic oriental seasoning made of roasted sesame seeds and sea salt, used mainly in Japan with rice and salads.

serve with
AMBER ALE

styleburger

difficulty	patty	season	inspiration	condiment
EASY	SCOTTONA BEEF	SUMMER	ITALY	CAPRINO SAUCE

1	**bun**
1	**Scottona beef patty 180 g**
3 slices	**bacon**
30 g	**Piacentinu cheese from Enna with saffron and pepper**
1 sprig	**wild arugula**
30 g	**Caprino cheese**
1	**firm fig**
2 leaves	**basil**
	balsamic vinegar matured 24 months
	butter
	extra-virgin olive oil
	black pepper

You can prepare the crispy bacon either by arranging the slices on a plate lined with oven paper and roast under the grill as desired, or roast them in a skillet without oil or butter: the bacon fat will melt and make the bacon crispy and flavorful.

Mix the Caprino with a little olive oil, pepper and a spoonful of warm water.

Lightly brush the patty with oil and place it on the heated grill to cook as desired.

Meanwhile, cut the fig in half, grill and season with pepper.

Cut the bun in half, spread a little softened butter on the cut sides and nonstick skillet till well browned.

Put the base of the bun on a cutting board, and add the arugula, the patty, the Caprino sauce, the grilled fig, the Piacentinu and the bacon with a trickle of balsamic vinegar. Finally spread the other half of the bun with the remaining Caprino sauce. Cover and use a cocktail stick to pin everything together.

special guest
PIACENTINU CHEESE FROM ENNA

A Sicilian ewe's milk cheese, spiked with saffron and black pepper, with a highly aromatic, slightly spicy taste.

serve with
PALE LAGER BEER

blessburger

difficulty	patty	season	inspiration	condiment
EASY	CHICKEN	SPRING	ITALY / NORTH AMERICA	PEANUT SAUCE

1	bun
1	chicken patty 180 g
30 g	Fontina DOP cheese
1 slice	Sorrento beefsteak tomato
1 sprig	wild arugula
1	whole leek
30 g	peanut sauce
	butter
	extra-virgin olive oil

Make the peanut sauce (see "Sauces").
Slice the white part of the leek into julienne strips and then keep them in water and ice.
Carefully wash the wild arugula.
Brush the patty lightly and put it on the heated grill until well done. Cover the patty with the Fontina cheese julienned, then cover with the lid until it melts slightly.
Cut the bun in half, spread the cut sides with a little softened butter and brown in a nonstick skillet.
Place the base of the bun on a cutting board with a little peanut sauce, then arrange the filling in the following order: the patty, arugula, leek and tomato.
Spread the other half of the bun with the rest of the peanut sauce and cover the burger. Pin everything together with a cocktail stick.

special guests
FONTINA VALDOSTANA DOP

A classic Italian cheese classified as made with semi-raw paste, produced exclusively from unpasteurized whole milk from cows raised In the Val d'Aosta.

 serve with
PALE LAGER BEER

starburger

difficulty	patty	season	inspiration	condimenti
MEDIUM	SCOTTONA BEEF	SUMMER	GREECE	TZAZIKI SAUCE

	bun
1	Scottona beef patty 180 g
1 slice	Sorrento beefsteak tomato
1 bunch	wild arugula
30 g	Feta cheese
2/3 rings	red onion
1	eggplant
1 clove	garlic
30 g	tzatziki sauce
	fresh thyme
	butter
	extra-virgin olive oil
	fine salt

Prepare the tzatziki sauce (see "Sauces").
Carefully trim and wash the arugula.
Make an eggplant carpaccio by removing all the peel, cutting the pulp into thin slices and cooking them in a well heated nonstick skillet. Arrange the slices in a bowl with a whole clove of garlic, the thyme, a pinch of salt and trickle of oil.
Brush the patty lightly with oil and cook it on the heated grill as desired.
Meanwhile, cut the bun in half, spread a little softened butter on the cut sides and brown in a nonstick skillet.
Put the base of the bun on a cutting board and add the arugula, the patty, the tomato, the eggplant carpaccio, the onion and finally the crumbled Feta cheese. Spread the other half of the bun with the tzatziki sauce and cover the burger. Pin everything together with a cocktail stick.

serve with
PALE LAGER BEER

 special guest
TZATZIKI SAUCE

The tzatziki that inspired this gourmet sauce is a condiment made from yogurt, typically Greek and common in the southern Balkans.

chickburger

difficulty
MEDIUM

patty
CHICKEN

season
SPRING

inspiration
ITALY / CENTRAL AMERICA

condiment
KETCHUP

1	**bun**
1	**chicken patty 180 g**
1 slice	**artisanal smoked roasted ham**
2 slices	**Cheddar cheese**
1 slice	**Sorrento beefsteak tomato**
1 leaf	**lettuce**
to taste	**green tabasco**
30 g	**ketchup**
	butter
	extra-virgin olive oil

Brush the patty lightly with oil and put it on the heated grill until cooked as desired.
Place the Cheddar over the patty, cover with the lid and let it melt.
Cut the bun in half, spread the cut sides with a little softened butter, and brown in a nonstick skillet.
Then put the base of the bun on a cutting board and add the lettuce, the tomato and the patty, two drops of green tabasco and top with the ham. Cover with the other half of the bun sprinkled with ketchup. Pin everything together using a cocktail stick.

special guest
ARTISANAL SMOKED ROASTED HAM

Artisanal Italian ham, cooked slowly for 8 hours, with no traces of polyphosphates, thickeners, casein or lactose.

serve with
SPICY BEER

wiseburger

difficulty
EASY

patty
PORK

season
4 SEASONS

inspiration
AFRICA / FUSION

condiment
HARISSA SAUCE

1	**bun**
1	**pork patty 180 g**
	stick chips
1	**lettuce heart**
2–3 rings	**red onion**
40 g	**Greek yogurt**
1 leaf	**basil**
30 g	**harissa sauce**
	butter
	extra-virgin olive oil

Make the stick chips according to the recipe (see "Fries").

Wash the lettuce heart and julienne it.

Mix the yogurt with a drizzle of olive oil and a chopped basil leaf.

Lightly brush the patty with oil and cook it on the heated grill as desired.

Meanwhile, cut the bun in half, spread the two cut sides with a little softened butter and brown them in a nonstick pan.

Put the base of the bun on a cutting board and arrange the burger, beginning with half the julienned lettuce, then the patty, a spoonful of basil yogurt, the onion, a handful of fries, the harissa and the rest of the lettuce. Cover the burger and use a cocktail stick to pin everything together.

special guest
HARISSA SAUCE

From the North-African culinary tradition,
a typical spicy sauce made of tomatoes and fresh chili.

serve with
MORELLINO RED WINE

simpletartar

difficulty
MEDIUM

tartare
SCOTTONA BEEF

season
4 SEASONS

inspiration
ITALY

condiment
WORCESTERSHIRE SAUCE

180 g	**Scottona beef fillet**
1	**egg**
1 handful	**capers**
1	**spring onion**
15 g	**Parmigiano Reggiano 24 months**
1 sprig	**parsley**
1	**lemon**
	old-style mustard
	Worcestershire sauce
	extra-virgin olive oil
	fleur de sel
	black peppercorns

Wipe the meat and cut it into fairly thin slices, then into strips. Finally chop it with a knife to make a tartar. Add a trickle of olive oil, a pinch of pepper, a few drops of Worcestershire sauce and mix all together gently.

There are two ways to season the tartar. In classic fashion, put the tartar in a dish using a greased round pastry cutter with a diameter of 10 cm and make a dimple in the middle to insert the egg yolk and Parmigiano shavings. Then in small bowls place separately the desalted capers (chopped lightly), the parsley, the spring onion and the mustard as desired.

Alternatively, season by mixing the chopped meat with the egg, capers, chopped spring onion and parsley, and serve all together using a round pastry cutter. Slip off the ring, garnish with Parmigiano flakes, grated lemon zest, a few flakes of salt and a pinch of peppercorns.

serve with
AMBER ALE

youthburger

difficulty	patty	season	inspiration	condiment
MEDIUM	SCOTTONA BEEF	SUMMER	ITALY	CAPER MAYONNAISE

1	**bun**
1	**Scottona beef patty 180 g**
30 g	**Parmigiano Reggiano 24 months**
2 slices	**Prosciutto Crudo di Parma**
	18 months Doppia Corona
1 sprig	**wild arugula**
1	**whole leek**
30 g	**caper mayonnaise**
	butter
	extra-virgin olive oil

Make the caper mayonnaise (see "Sauces").

Heat a nonstick skillet, sprinkle the Parmigiano in it then let it melt and form a golden crust. Use kitchen tongs to flip over the wafer that formed to brown the other side. When ready let it cool.

Julienne the white part of the leek and keep it in water and ice. Then carefully trim and wash the arugula. Brush the patty lightly with oil, put it on the heated grill and cook as desired.

Meanwhile, cut the bun in half, spread the cut sides with softened butter and brown the two halves in a nonstick pan.

Put the base of the bun on a cutting board and add the arugula, the patty, the Parmigiano wafer, julienned leeks and finally the Prosciutto. Spread the caper mayonnaise on the top half of the bun and close the burger. Pin everything together with a cocktail stick.

special guest
PROSCIUTTO CRUDO DI PARMA DOPPIA CORONA

Among the finest Italian hams, Prosciutto Crudo Doppia Corona seasoned 18 months comes from farms in the Langhirano area in the province of Parma.

serve with
INDIA PALE ALE

beatburger

difficulty
MEDIUM

patty
SCOTTONA BEEF

season
AUTUMN

inspiration
ITALY

condiment
HONEY AND GREEN
PEPPER SAUCE

1	**bun**
1	**Scottona beef patty 180 g**
100 g	**oyster mushrooms**
30 g	**Caciocavallo Podolico**
20 g	**Guanciale di Norcia**
	(Norcia pork cheek)
2 leaves	**radicchio**
40 g	**honey and green pepper sauce**
1 clove	**garlic**
	mountain oregano
	butter
	extra-virgin olive oil
	fine salt
	pepper

Prepare the honey and green pepper sauce (see "Sauces").

Make an aromatic seasoning by mixing the extra-virgin olive oil, chopped garlic, salt, oregano and pepper.

Remove the woody base of the mushrooms, grill on both sides, then season with the aromatic oil.

Brush a little oil on the patty, put it on the heated grill and cook as desired.

Meanwhile, cut the bun in half, spread a little butter on the inner sides and brown the two halves in a skillet.

Once they are brown put the base of the bun on a cutting board and cover with the julienned radicchio, the patty, the Guanciale sliced, the flakes of Cacciacavallo and the mushrooms. Trickle over a little of the honey and green pepper sauce and finally smear the other half of the bun with the rest. Cover and pin everything together with a cocktail stick.

serve with
RED BEER

funburger

difficulty
MEDIUM

patty
SCOTTONA BEEF

season
WINTER

inspiration
ITALY

condiment
GREEN PEPPER SAUCE

1	bun
1	Scottona beef patty 180 g
15 g	mature Gorgonzola
2 slices	Italian Speck
2 leaves	spumiglia lettuce
30 g	green pepper sauce
1	artichoke
1 clove	garlic
½	lemon
1 sprig	parsley
	chestnut honey
	butter
	extra-virgin olive oil
	fine salt

Prepare the green pepper sauce (see "Sauces").

Clean the artichoke, trim it carefully, remove the inner "choke" or beard and then slice it. Keep the slices in water acidulated with lemon.

In a pan warm the oil and fry the garlic lightly, then remove it when golden. Add the artichoke and cook it for 1 minute, then cover with the lid and cook for about 2 minutes longer; season with salt and add the chopped parsley. Keep it warm.

Brush a little oil on the patty, put it on the heated grill and cook as desired.

Put the Gorgonzola on the patty and cover with the lid to melt it slightly.

Meanwhile, cut the bun in half, spread the cut sides with softened butter and put them in a pan to brown lightly.

Put the base of the bun on a cutting board, place the spumiglia lettuce leaf on it, then the patty, artichoke and Speck with a trickle of honey. Spread the other half of the bun with the green pepper sauce and cover the burger. Use a cocktail stick to pin everything together.

serve with
BOCK BEER

pureburger

difficulty
MEDIUM

patty
SEITAN

season
SPRING / SUMMER

inspiration
INDIA / CHINA

condiment
TOFU AND CURRY SAUCE

1	bun
1	seitan patty
1	whole leek
3 slices	tomato
1 leaf	lettuce
40 g	tofu and curry sauce
	butter
	extra-virgin olive oil

Prepare the tofu and curry sauce (see "Sauces").
Slice the white of the leek into julienne strips and keep them in water and ice.
Brush the patty with oil and put in a very hot skillet till done.
Meanwhile, cut the bun in half, spread the cut sides with a little butter and brown them in a nonstick skillet.
Put the base of the bun on a cutting board and cover it with a little sauce. Then add the lettuce, tomatoes, seitan patty, the rest of the curry and tofu sauce and the leek. Cover the bun. Pin the ingredients together with a cocktail stick.

serve with
GINGER BEER

deepburger

difficulty
EASY

patty
SCOTTONA BEEF

season
WINTER

inspiration
ITALY / FRANCE

condimenti
GREEN PEPPER
SAUCE

1	**bun**
1	**Scottona beef patty 180 g**
20 f	**Brie cheese**
1	**small artichoke**
2 foglie	**radicchio**
20 g	**green pepper sauce**
	butter
	extra-virgin olive oil
	salt
	black pepper

Prepare the green pepper sauce (see "Sauces").
Cut the artichoke into thin slices and dress it with a drizzle of olive oil, salt and black pepper.
Brush the patty lightly with oil, put it on the hot grill and cook as desired.
Meanwhile, cut the bun in half, spread a little softened butter on the two cut sides and brown it in a nonstick skillet.
Put the base of the bun on a cutting board, add the radicchio julienned, the patty, Brie and artichoke slices.
Spread the other half of the bun with green pepper sauce and cover the burger.
Pin everything together with a cocktail stick.

serve with
AMBER RED BEER

gladburger

difficulty	patty	season	inspiration	condiment
MEDIUM	SCOTTONA BEEF	4 SEASONS	MOROCCO	YOGURT SAUCE

1	**bun**
1	**Scottona beef patty 180 g**
1 slice	**Sorrento beefsteak tomato**
1 leaf	**lettuce**
2–3 rings	**red onion**
30 g	**yogurt sauce**
	cumin powder
	butter
	extra-virgin olive oil
	hummus
200 g	**cooked chickpeas**
1 clove	**garlic**
1 spoonful	**tahini (sesame cream)**
½	**lemon**
1 spoonful	**cumin powder**
1 sprig	**fresh cilantro**
20 g	**extra-virgin olive oil**

Prepare the yogurt sauce (see "Sauces").
To make the hummus, warm the oil with the garlic, add the cumin powder and boiled chickpeas and sauté together for a few minutes. Pour into the blender cup adding the juice of half a lemon and a spoonful of tahini. Blend in short bursts, adding a trickle of oil or a spoonful of hot water to give it a creamy consistency.
Chop the cilantro with a knife and mix with the hummus.
Brush the patty lightly with oil, place on the heated grill and cook as desired, then season it with a sprinkling of cumin.
Meanwhile, cut the bun in half, lightly spread the cut sides with butter and brown in a skillet.
Put the base of the bun on a cutting board and add the tomato, lettuce and onion, with a trickle of olive oil, the patty and finally add a spoonful of hummus Spread the other half of the bun with the yogurt sauce and close the burger. Pin everything together with a cocktail stick.

special guest
HUMMUS

Its origin is lost in the antiquity of the Arab world, but today it is also used in international cuisine. Made from chickpeas and various seasonings, it is deliciously creamy and even a piece of bread dipped in it makes a delicious snack.

serve with
WEIZEN BEER

rockburger

difficulty
MEDIUM

patty
PORK

season
WINTER

inspiration
ITALY

condiment
HOLY SAUCE

1	**bun**
1	**pork patty 180 g**
2 slices	**Sorrento smoked Scamorza cheese**
1 slice	**Sorrento beefsteak tomato**
1 sprig	**wild arugula**
30 g	**eggplant fillets in olive oil**
30 g	**holy sauce**
	butter
	extra-virgin olive oil

Make the holy sauce (see "Sauces").
Carefully trim and wash the arugula.
Brush the patty lightly with oil, put it on the heated grill and cook as desired. Put the slices of smoked cheese on the patty and cover them with the lid so they melt.
Meanwhile, cut the bun in two and spread the cut sides with a little softened butter and brown them in a skillet.
On a cutting board begin to assemble the burger by putting a little holy sauce on the base of the bun, then the arugula, tomato, the patty and the eggplant fillets. Spread the other half of the bread with the holy sauce and close the bun. Pin everything together with a cocktail stick.

serve with
MORELLINO RED WINE

Discovering new things, trying different approaches, imagining the unexpected, approaching unimaginable things: these are the best things in life. That's how all these recipes came to be.

LIFE IS BEAUTIFUL

When you enter a Ham you instantly make contact with its world and its philosophy. Concepts, visual elements and materials are assembled in contemporary architectures, where the modern style blends seamlessly with the roots and histories of places. Technology makes it possible to provide an interactive service, superfast and efficient, without losing any of the goodness, safety and freshness that are always all-important. This can be seen in the glass-fronted counter with a view of the dishes being prepared, in the chilled tanks of soft drinks and beers and also in the kitchen thanks to a live cam always active that can be viewed by every patron. New technological applications are provided to enable you to book a table, order or pre-order even before you get to the restaurant. Or for seeing the recipes, finding out more about the ingredients and their preparation, entering the community and enjoying special promotions, but also simply so you can connect yourself online with the world and have a great time, enjoy your leisure.

THAT'S WHAT I HAM
Duty foremost, but your pleasure first of all.

Ham is always abuzz with ideas. On the one hand continuously studying gourmet taste trends to create seasonal menus, because the recipes change to reflect the availability of the finest specialties, and on the other devising ever new ideas for having unforgettable experiences in his restaurants.

Log in to Ham Holy Burger at
www.hamholyburger.it

ham
holy burger

SCOTTONA BEEF

1 **holy**burger
with tomato, cucumber, onion, lettuce and holy sauce

45 **beat**burger
with mushrooms, Caciocavallo Podolico, Guanciale di Norcia, radicchio and honey and green pepper sauce

30 **black**burger
with mushrooms, Provolone Auricchio cheese, bacon, lettuce and BBQ sauce

2 **club**burger
with Caciocavallo Podolico, zucchini, arugula and Stracchino cheese sauce

9 **cult**burger
with spinach, lettuce, leeks, hazelnuts, and green pepper and juniper mayonnaise

48 **deep**burger
with Brie cheese, artichoke, radicchio and green pepper sauce

12 **early**burger
with Bûche de chèvre, black truffle, tomato, Prosciutto Crudo, onion, gentilina lettuce and old-style mustard mayonnaise

36 **faith**burger
with 'Nduja Calabrese, smoked Scamorza cheese, tomato, onion, iceberg lettuce and barbecue sauce

13 **feel**burger
with Cheddar cheese, roasted ham, pineapple, radicchio and green tomato chutney

46 **fun**burger
with Gorgonzola cheese, Speck, artichoke, spumiglia lettuce and green pepper sauce

20 **gift**burger
with Guanciale di Norcia, Tuscan Pecorino cheese, spinach, mustard mayonnaise and walnut pesto

49 **glad**burger
with tomato, lettuce, onion, hummus and yogurt sauce

16 **heart**burger
with roasted ham, Parmigiano Reggiano, mushrooms, radicchio, and peanut sauce

26 **holyxmas**burger
with radicchio, bacon, sauté of chestnuts, mushrooms, Melannurca and rosemary sauce

6 **keep**burger
with Bûche de chèvre, Speck, spumiglia lettuce, fig, sauté of onions and rosemary sauce

27 **kid**burger
with Cheddar cheese, chips, ketchup and mayonnaise

24 **land**burger
with ratatouille, lettuce, black olives, dried tomatoes, Scamorza cheese and holy sauce

31 **legend**burger
with smoked Provola cheese, tomato, eggplant, zucchini, bell pepper and basil mayonnaise

5 **lounge**burger
with Prosciutto Crudo, Provolone Auricchio cheese, mushrooms, lettuce, truffle oil and green pepper sauce

15 **peak**burger
with Jerusalem artichoke chips, arugula, roasted ham, Parmigiano Reggiano and old-style mustard mayonnaise

34 **rising**burger
with Feta cheese, creamed eggplant, lettuce and balsamic vinegar ketchup

35 **skill**burger
with Prosciutto Crudo, Parmigiano Reggiano, spinach, mushrooms and truffle mayonnaise

29 **smart**burger
with roasted ham, tomato, arugula, mango, onion and wasabi sauce

17 **soul**burger
with Cheddar cheese, bacon, egg, tomato, lettuce, cucumber, onion, relish sauce and barbecue sauce

37 **sound**burger
with Caprino cheese, bell peppers, iceberg lettuce, black olive tapenade, sesame salt and holy sauce

40 **star**burger
with tomato, arugula, Feta cheese, onion, eggplant and tzatziki sauce

38 **style**burger
with bacon, Sicilian Piacentinu cheese with saffron and pepper, arugula, fig, Caprino cheese sauce

19 **sunday**burger
with arugula, Parmigiano Reggiano, lime, rum and mint yogurt

22 **touch**burger
with roasted ham, buffalo-milk Gorgonzola cheese, gentilina lettuce, radicchio, onion, redcurrant glaze, grappa and barbecue sauce

43 **youth**burger
with Prosciutto Crudo, arugula, leek, Parmigiano Reggiano and caper mayonnaise

SCOTTONA BEEF TARTAR

18 fusiontartar
with bell pepper, tomato, avocado, onion and tartar sauce

43 simpletartar
with egg, capers, spring onion, Parmigiano Reggiano, parsley, old-style mustard and Worcestershire sauce

PORK

14 easyburger
with smoked Scamorza cheese, tomato, lettuce, onion and barbecue sauce

3 goodyburger
with sauté of sweet or sour cherries, Doomstone cheese cream with bourbon, radicchio, onion and smoked barbecue sauce

50 rockburger
with smoked Scamorza cheese, tomatoes, arugula, eggplant fillets and holy sauce

10 spicyburger
with arugula, Leicester cheese, bacon, green chili, pineapple and spicy ketchup sauce

42 wiseburger
chips, lettuce, onion and Greek yogurt with harissa

CHICKEN

39 blessburger
with Fontina DOP cheese, tomato, arugula, leek and peanut sauce

41 chickburger
with roasted ham, Cheddar cheese, tomato, lettuce, green tabasco and ketchup

4 gleeburger
with Cheddar cheese, roasted ham, colorful salad with mayonnaise, arugula with citrus mayonnaise

25 slightburger
with Emmentaler AOC, tomatoes, arugula and carrot and cumin mayonnaise

28 whiteburger
with roasted ham, Scamorza cheese, tomato, lettuce, onion and curry sauce

VEGETARIAN

32 freeburger
seitan patty, tomato, lettuce, eggplant and basil mayonnaise

23 greenburger
patty with potatoes, zucchini and carrots, iceberg lettuce, spring onion, basil pesto and yoghurt sauce

47 pureburger
seitan patty, leek, tomato, lettuce and tofu curry sauce

7 veggyburger
millefeuille of grilled vegetables, Scamorza cheese and basil mayonnaise

FISH

8 hugeburger
tuna patty with black olives, fennel, spring onion, orange and caper mayonnaise

33 jewelburger
lobster patty with bell pepper, cherry tomatoes, arugula and citrus mayonnaise

21 riseburger
salmon patty, green chili, lime, tomato, lettuce, onion and yogurt and mustard mayonnaise

11 upperburger
shrimp patty, iceberg lettuce, carpaccio of zucchini and curry sauce

VOLUME CONVERSIONS: NORMALLY USED FOR LIQUIDS ONLY

Metric equivalent	Customary quantity
5 g/ml	1 teaspoon (tsp)
15 g/ml	1 tablespoon (tbsp) *or* 1/2 fluid ouncetbsp
30 ml	1 fluid ounce *or* 1/8 cup
60 ml	1/4 cup *or* 2 fluid ounces
80 ml	1/3 cup
120 ml	1/2 cup *or* 4 fluid ounces
160 ml	2/3 cup
180 ml	3/4 cup *or* 6 fluid ounces
240 ml	1 cup *or* 8 fluid ounces *or* half a pint
350 ml	1 1/2 cups *or* 12 fluid ounces
475 ml	2 cups *or* 1 pint *or* 16 fluid ounces
700 ml	3 cups *or* 1 1/2 pints
950 ml	4 cups *or* 2 pints *or* 1 quart

Note: In cases where higher precision is not justified, it may be convenient to round these conversions off as follows:

250 ml	1 cup
500 ml	1 pint
1 l	1 quart
4 l	1 gallon

Weight Conversions

Metric equivalent	Customary quantity
28 g	1 ounce
113 g	4 ounces *or* 1/4 pound
150 g	1/3 pound
230 g	8 ounces *or* 1/2 pound
300 g	2/3 pound
340 g	12 ounces *or* 3/4 pound
450 g	1 pound *or* 16 ounces
900 g	2 pounds

WEIGHTS OF COMMON INGREDIENTS IN GRAMS

Baking Powder	15 g	1 tbsp
	5 g	1 tsp
Baking Soda	15 g	1 tbsp
	5 g	1 tsp
Butter	240 g	1 cup
	30 g	1 tbsp
Corn Meal	160 g	1 cup
Corn Starch	130 g	1 cup
Egg, medium size	5 units	1 cup
	275 g	
Egg yolk, medium size	12 units	1 cup
	300 g	
Egg white, medium size	8 units	1 cup
	240 g	
Flour, all purpose	120 g	1 cup
Flour, Almond	100 g	1 cup
Flour, Bread	120 g	1 cup
Flour, Cake	110 g	1 cup
Flour, Gluten free Multi-purpose	150 g	1 cup
Flour, Rice	140 g	1 cup
Flour, Whole Wheat	115 g	1 cup
Fruits and vegetables, chopped	150 g	1 cup
Honey	340 g	1 cup
	20 g	1 tbsp
Mayonnaise	230 g	1 cup
Milk	245 g	1 cup
	250 ml	
Oil	200 g	1 cup
	222 ml	
Parmesan cheese, grated	90 g	1 cup
	11 g	2 tbsp
Potato Starch	150 g	1 cup
Salt	40 g	2 tbsp
Sugar, brown	220 g	1 cup
	14 g	1 tbsp
	5 g	1 tsp

Sugar, confectioner	120 g	1 cup
	8 g	1tbsp
	3 g	1 tsp
Sugar, white	200 g	1 cup
	12 g	1 tbsp
	4 g	1 tsp
Vegetable shortening	190 g	1 cup
Water	235 g	1 cup
	235 ml	
Yeast, active dry	10 g	1 tbsp
	3 g	1 tsp
Yeast, fresh	10 g	1 tbsp
	3 g	1 tsp
Yogurt	245 g	1 cup
	250 ml	

Oven temperature

°Fahrenheit	Gas Mark	°Celsius
250	1/2	120
275	1	140
300	2	150
325	3	165
350	4	180
375	5	190
400	6	200
425	7	220
450	8	230
475	9	240
500	10	260
550	Broil	290

Unless otherwise specified, all oven temperatures in this book are for conventional (static) ovens.
For convection (fan-assisted) ovens, decrease the oven temperature by 25°F (20°C)
and bake for approximately the same amount of time, but monitor closely as convection
ovens can cook more efficiently. Ovens vary, so calibrate yours frequently for best results.

Behind every great initiative there's always a bright creative mind. Two minds in this case. Because Ham Holy Burger is the brainchild of two outstanding chefs, ANTONIO SORRENTINO and ENZO DE ANGELIS. Their intuition, experience and research lie behind all the recipes, choice of ingredients, methods of preparation and gourmet combinations. They made possible this absolutely unique and original journey into taste which grew out of their passion. As authors, researchers, writers, guests on numerous TV shows, profound connoisseurs of gourmet food and wine, chefs and friends. The pleasure you feel as you make and taste each recipe is above all else what they wanted for you.

ONE WORLD
TWO MINDS
FOUR HANDS

HOLY STAFF

gourmet chefs
ANTONIO SORRENTINO
ENZO DE ANGELIS

project manager
ROSELÌ KATIBE

graphic designer
GIORGIA MELE

photographs by
MAURIZIO DE FAZIO
QUID & QUID srl

copywriter
SIMONE NATALI